What people are saying about …

GREATER JOY TWOGETHER

"With two decades of ministry and marriage tools under his belt, my friend Ted shares pro tips on *relational* construction and renovation in this excellent new book. He drills down on the importance of building a strong foundation through prayer, communication, affirmation, and teamwork. At the same time, he encourages couples to carve out space for laughter, intimacy, and refreshment. If you're looking for some fresh ideas to improve your marriage, this is the book for you!"

Greg Smalley, PsyD, vice president of
marriage at Focus on the Family

"Ted Cunningham walks the talk. Whether he is onstage for his renowned Comedy Date Night events, preaching at his amazing church in Branson, or writing one of his bestselling marriage books, Ted is the real deal— authentic, grounded, and practical. Oh, and funny too. He will make you laugh while you learn. If you're looking for weekly inspiration in your marriage, not to mention deeper joy, don't miss out on this beautiful devotional book."

Drs. Les and Leslie Parrott, #1 *New York Times*–bestselling
authors of *Saving Your Marriage Before It Starts*

"*Greater Joy TWOgether* is the most *enjoyable* marriage book I have ever read. I literally laughed out loud many times. Even better, there's an abundance of wise counsel and seasoned insight to help any couple draw closer together."

Gary Thomas, author of *Sacred Marriage,*
Cherish, and *A Lifelong Love*

"Ted Cunningham is one of my favorite people, and *Greater Joy TWOgether* will quickly become your favorite weekly devotional. With Ted's signature humor, practicality, and wisdom, this book walks couples through Scripture, special times of conversation, and prayer. This journey will bring great joy to every marriage."

Shaunti Feldhahn, social researcher and bestselling
author of *For Women Only* and *For Men Only*

"I love how *Greater Joy TWOgether* biblically and practically helps couples connect with each other and with God. Spiritual intimacy is often the least developed area of intimacy in marriage, and simply spending twenty minutes a week together can change that for you."

Jim Burns, PhD, president of HomeWord,
author of *Creating an Intimate*
Marriage, and coauthor of *Closer*

"Full of wisdom, fun, practical advice, and a boatload of humor, *Greater Joy TWOgether* will bless and strengthen any marriage. I highly recommend this book for anyone seeking a deeper, fuller, richer, understanding of biblical marriage in the midst of a broken world. I also recommend this book to anyone in need of a good belly laugh."

Jimmy Dodd, founder and CEO of PastorServe,
coauthor of *What Great Ministry Leaders Get*
Right and *The Magnificent Names of Jesus*

"This book gives couples a GPS that guides them step by step from the beginning of their relationship journey through their lifetime, laughing all the way."

Dr. Yakov Smirnoff, comedian

"So much practical packed into 52 weeks! Go slow, talk about it, pray about it, and watch where God leads you in your marriage. *Greater Joy TWOgether* is a difference maker for marriages."

Julie Baumgardner, MS, CFLE, senior director, WinShape Marriage

"Besides being an excellent storyteller, Ted gives couples practical questions to talk about, suggestions of things to do, and prompts to pray together. The best marriages include laughter, shared experiences, and community with others who will cheer you on. Reading this book is an easy step toward making our marriages better in 52 weeks."

Jána Guynn, director of marrieds, Gwinnett Church, North Point Ministries

"Ted's heart for the Lord, for his church, and for the family permeates this 52-week devotional for couples. From humor to Scripture to practical action steps to focused prayers, *Greater Joy TWOgether* gives husbands and wives a weekly road map to staying focused and intentional in their marriage!"

Clay Cunningham, next generation pastor, First Baptist Church, Benton, Arkansas

"Ted Cunningham's new marriage devotional, *Greater Joy TWOgether*, is a book I will be recommending to couples—no matter how long they've been married! It's engaging, fun, and full of action steps and discussion questions that will deepen your relationships with both your spouse and the Lord. Commit to going through this book together (or *two-gether*)!"

Tom Henderson, RESGEN founder, speaker, author, and RESGEN *Giving Life* podcast host

"Ted has delivered an encouraging, practical, and energizing devotional book for couples. With his trademark humor and fresh insights, every couple should commit a year of their marriage to reading *Greater Joy TWOgether*."

Roger Gibson, marriage pastor, Fellowship of the Parks

"Overflowing with Ted's uplifting and refreshing brand of storytelling, this 52-week devotional combines all of Ted's greatest teaching and comedy nuggets into one easy-to-read collection. *Greater Joy TWOgether* is a must-have resource for any couple looking for a fun, thought-provoking, and engaging way to enrich their marriage."

Barry Ford, minister to young married adults, First Baptist Dallas

"As you read *Greater Joy TWOgether*, I know you will be refreshed by Ted's unique blend of real-life talk, incredible sense of humor, and Jesus-centered solutions. On top of that, you will be equipped with practical ways to talk, live, and pray the principles you learn together."

Chip Henderson, senior pastor, Pinelake Church

"With Ted's sense of humor leaping off the page, *Greater Joy TWOgether* will make you and your spouse laugh together, learn biblical principles together, and most of all, grow closer together as you make your marriage all God desires it to be."

Jarrett Stephens, senior pastor, Champion Forest Baptist Church and author of *The Always God*

"*Greater Joy TWOgether* is Christ-centered, biblical, honest, practical, and funny. You will love your marriage more, your spouse more, and most importantly, you'll love Jesus more."

Scott Kedersha, marriage pastor, Harris Creek
Baptist Church and author of *Ready or Knot?*

"Thoroughly enjoyed *Greater Joy TWOgether*. Excellent resource that is timely, practical, and stimulating for any marriage."

Don Blackmore, adult discipleship pastor,
Central Baptist, Jonesboro, Arkansas

"My wife and I so enjoyed Ted's practical mix of relatable stories and rich marriage activities wrapped together with prompts for reflection, prayer, and action. Couples who use this devotional will have fun, become greater friends, and deepen in their discipleship."

J. P. De Gance, president and CEO, Communio

"Not only does Ted have a great marriage, but he studies the essential elements of a healthy marriage and writes with conviction and hope. I highly recommend that you read this with your spouse so you'll grow, laugh, and keep your marriage from drifting."

Doug Fields, author of *7 Ways to Be Her Hero*

"Ted's process is enjoyable, and his purpose is biblical. In other words, *Greater Joy TWOgether* is a faithful and fun endeavor. I like it and you will too! It's a doable devotional."

Dennis Swanberg, "America's Minister of Encouragement"

GREATER
JOY
TWOGETHER

A 52-WEEK MARRIAGE
DEVOTIONAL

TED CUNNINGHAM

DAVID C COOK®

transforming lives together

GREATER JOY TWOGETHER
Published by David C Cook
4050 Lee Vance Drive
Colorado Springs, CO 80918 U.S.A.

Integrity Music Limited, a Division of David C Cook
Brighton, East Sussex BN1 2RE, England

The graphic circle C logo is a registered trademark of David C Cook.

Library of Congress Control Number 2023931060
ISBN 978-0-8307-8527-8
eISBN 978-0-8307-8528-5

© 2023 Ted Cunningham
Published in association with The Bindery Agency, www.TheBinderyAgency.com.

The Team: Susan McPherson, Stephanie Bennett, Jeff Gerke, Judy
Gillispie, Leigh Davidson, James Hershberger, Susan Murdock
Cover Design: Juicebox Designs

Printed in the United States of America
First Edition 2023

1 2 3 4 5 6 7 8 9 10

050923

To Corynn and Caden Hazell,

I rejoice and delight in your young, budding love.
Your mom and I pray for you every day.
You bring great joy to those around you.
Your future together is bright.
I love you.

CONTENTS

ACKNOWLEDGMENTS

David C Cook, this is our fourth book together. From start to finish, the entire team is professional, kind, fun, and Christ-honoring. You stand by your authors, and for that I am grateful. Susan McPherson and Stephanie Bennett walked with me every step of the way on this book. Thank you for believing in this project and helping couples enjoy life together. Thank you, Jeff Gerke. You are an encouraging editor. More than your edits, I enjoyed your instruction. You made me a better writer.

Ingrid Beck and Alex Field are more than literary agents—they are trusted friends. We've worked together for more than ten years now. I look forward to many more books together.

Shaunti Feldhahn, Gary Thomas, and Les Parrott, you three are a constant encouragement to me in marriage ministry. Thank you for being my friends and for being only a phone call or text away.

My friends at our 2022 Live the Adventure Alaska Retreat were the first readers of the unedited manuscript of this book. Thank you to Todd and Kristie Riggins, Tom and Denise Boerema, Travis and Kari Brawner, Brad Hunter, Julie Jackson, Warren and Mandy Rogers, Del Nordby, Robyn Mitchell, Doug and Dee Goodwin, Scott and Lynn Rhoda, RG and Karen Yallaly, Gary and Lisa Stewart, Mark and Sandi Larson, Steve and Dawn Larson, and Lindsey Larson. Thank you for hearing me out and offering feedback. A very special thank-you to

Gary and Lisa Stewart, Mark and Sandi Larson, and Lindsey Larson for hosting this Alaskan adventure. Your hospitality is second to none.

Woodland Hills Family Church, thank you for graciously allowing me to serve marriages and families outside of the Ozarks. I will not be your pastor forever, but I have asked the Lord to allow me to die as a member of our church. If it is the Lord's will, I plan on being an old man at the early service cheering on the lead pastor, staff, and congregation. I love our church.

Corynn Hazell, you were the first one to read through the manuscript. Thank you for editing and cheering me on. I am proud of you and Caden!

Carson, you bring your dad great joy. I finished writing this book the day before you started your senior year of high school. I'm taking no writing projects until you go to college so we can knock out more games on our NBA stadium tour. Your mom and I love spending time with you.

Amy, the words of this book are the practice of our marriage. I know you say I keep our marriage fun, but you keep our marriage centered and grounded. You are the steadiest person I know. You lead with strength and integrity. Thank you for your unconditional love and support for me and everything I do.

INTRODUCTION

After twenty years of ministry to couples, my passion is greater and my message is more focused than ever on helping couples enjoy life together. I pray that the Lord gives me another forty years in this great work.

Whether speaking at marriage conferences or at our Date Night Comedy events, I want couples to laugh and learn as they grow in their relationship with the Lord and each other. That is my prayer for this 52-week devotional as well.

I am convinced now more than ever that couples need to lighten up and enjoy each other. Sometimes we make marriage harder than it needs to be. God did not give my spouse to me to be the primary challenge of my life but to be my companion through all the seasons and stages of life.

Newlyweds, seasoned couples, and couples in crisis will all learn something from these devotionals. Go through each one at your own pace. I hope each devotional sticks with you throughout the week. Talk about them when you get up, as you get ready, and when you share a meal or drive down the road. Read each one early in the week and discuss it throughout the rest of the week.

Share these devotionals with your friends, small group, or Sunday school class. They are for your marriage and the marriages around you. Yes, of course I want you to learn and grow, but I also want to equip you to help other couples. You are backup singers to the duets all around you. Use these devotionals to spark conversation during your next dinner out with friends.

Each devotional ends with three sections: "Let's TALK about It," "Let's DO Something about It," and "Let's PRAY about It." All three sections bring you into deeper devotion with God and each other.

> I want you to learn and grow, but I also want to equip you to help other couples. You are backup singers to the duets all around you.

There are many topics to read through and discuss together in this book. Amy and I have worked through each one over the past twenty-five years of marriage. Topics include humor, laughter, food, parenting, couple friends, sexual intimacy, communication, quality time, in-laws, finances, anger, forgiveness, and ministry to others. Every devotional and follow-up discussion is written to bring greater joy to your marriage.

Thank you for trusting me to invest in your marriage. I do not take this lightly. I prayed over each devotional, discussion question, activity, and prayer. I rejoice and delight in you and your marriage. I believe great days and greater joy are ahead for you and your spouse.

ENJOYING LIFE TOGETHER

*Enjoy life with your wife, whom you love, all the days of this meaningless
life that God has given you under the sun—all your meaningless days.
For this is your lot in life and in your toilsome labor under the sun.*

Ecclesiastes 9:9

God did not give you a spouse to be a grind that hinders you. He gave
you a spouse to accompany you *through* the grind of life. When your
spouse becomes the grind, your marriage drifts.

Most marriages start with two people enjoying life together. So
when someone tells me, "I'm not happy in my marriage," I hear, "We
don't have what we once did."

I am not one to respond with, "Marriage isn't about your happi-
ness," or "Marriage is hard … deal with it." I would rather paint a
beautiful picture of marriage, point the couple in the direction of
marital satisfaction, and provide practical steps toward enjoying
greater joy together.

Marital satisfaction is a choice, not an outcome. You cannot discover it online, and it will not find you after a series of serendipitous
events, as depicted in movies. It is based on decisions, factors, and
skills that couples can do something about in any season of life. You

decide your way into marital satisfaction by choosing it, or else you drift from it. Those are the only two options.

Dear friends of mine listened to me preach on marriage for six years before they had their first child. Several of my sermons had included the challenge to eradicate the kid-centered home. My friends would say to each other, "That will never happen to us. We will be careful to never have a kid-centered home!" Guess what? After the birth of their first child, everything changed. That child became the center of their universe. As my friend so eloquently put it, "We stopped being us." As a result, their marriage drifted from what they had once enjoyed.

Children certainly bring couples into new stages of life, and for some, it leads to marital drift. The seasons of life change us. Jobs, age, health struggles, pandemics, social unrest, and tragedy all contribute to this change. Some marriage experts believe that over the course of your marriage, it will seem like you had been married to five to seven different people. Enjoying life together requires that you do not turn your spouse into the grind but rather live in curiosity and fascination with the changes you see in each other.

Amy and I caught ourselves in drift in April of 2020. The COVID-19 pandemic had shut down the world a few weeks prior, and everything about our comfort and routine had come to a screeching halt.

As we sat in lawn chairs in our garage staring out into the woods, Amy asked me, "We're spending a lot of time together. Would you call it quality time?" That was the wake-up call we needed. When decisions we'd made for our marriage and family were tossed in the trash in March 2020, we, like most of the world, stopped making decisions for our future. We recognized drift that day and created a new path forward.

That's our desire for this devotional. For some, it will be a new discipline for your marriage. If you've never read or discussed the Bible together as a couple, start now. Maybe prayer other than at mealtime has never crossed your mind. I pray this devotional is where that spiritual discipline begins for your marriage. If you once read the Bible together and prayed together but now are in drift, there's no better time than the present to restart those practices. For many, this will foster a continuation of good habits you already have in place.

Wherever your marriage journey is right now, I pray this devotional is a pivotal resource that brings greater joy to your relationship with Jesus and each other.

Let's TALK about It

Discuss the following questions together, today or throughout the week.

- What season or stage of our marriage do we look back on with great joy?
- What was the most difficult season or stage?
- What are some big changes we navigated early in our marriage?
- Which ones brought us closer together and which ones led to drift?
- How quickly do we recognize drift?

Let's DO Something about It

To start, let's keep it simple. The following three decisions will get you started in this devotional time together. For each question below, circle the option that works best for you as a couple, and commit to that time and format for the next year.

1. We will read this devotional
   together / individually, then discuss.
2. We choose S M T W T F S as the best day
   of the week to read and discuss it.
3. The best time of the day for us to read it is
   morning / afternoon / evening.

Let's PRAY about It

Prioritizing prayer will bring you closer together and pave the way for God to work in your life and relationship. Use the following prayer as a jumping-off point.

Father, our desire is to glorify and enjoy you forever. We also want to enjoy each other. We will not allow the seasons and stages of life to determine our joy. We choose joy because we choose you and each other. Thank you for our marriage and for giving us one another to go through each season and stage of life with. We love you, and it is in the name of Jesus we pray. Amen.

OUR SHARED SENSE OF HUMOR

A cheerful heart is good medicine,
but a crushed spirit dries up the bones.

Proverbs 17:22

Making my wife laugh is part of my mission in life. Amy's laugh is truly something to witness. She goes silent, places her hand over her heart, leans forward, and stops breathing. I call it the silent, patriotic laugh.

After I tell her a particularly amusing joke or story, I'm careful to follow up with "Breathe, babe; breathe." I'm not always successful at making her let out a belly laugh, but I'll take a chuckle, cackle, or smile from her any day. Laughter keeps our marriage fresh and fun.

For example, twenty-five years of marriage have not stopped me from modeling my wardrobe for Amy as I get dressed each morning. I strut into the bathroom like a New York runway model and give my wife "the smolder." Have you seen the smolder? It's a tilt of the head, a raise of the left eyebrow, and a whimsical, sexy pucker of the lips. But trust me, when I do it, there is nothing sexy about it. Therein lies the humor.

Whether you have been married a few weeks or several decades, being intentional about the simple things, including shared laughter, is life giving. This is what fascinates me: If Amy and I are intentional, little connections begin to feel natural again. If we're not intentional, we drift apart. No one *chooses* to drift in marriage; drift sneaks in when we stop enjoying life together.

Most of the time, a good joke needs no introduction. One of the keys is the element of surprise. You don't want the other person to see the punch line coming.

But that's not my wife's method. She introduces her jokes and humorous stories with, "I'm going to tell you a joke," or "I need to share something funny that happened to me today." What she is really saying is "I need you to laugh after I tell you this."

Her approach is brilliant because it gets a double laugh. I laugh right away because her up-front request is humorous enough. And if the punch line isn't very funny, or if the joke is a repeat, I fake-laugh, and then we both crack up. We are so good at fake laughter and do it so often that it turns into genuine laughter soon enough.

Amy makes me laugh the most when she forces herself to laugh at my bad dad jokes. I tell them just so she can get the ball rolling with a forced chuckle. Laughter is contagious—even when it starts with a fake laugh.

Laughter helps us cope with difficult seasons and stages of life, but there is a time and place for joking. Amy and I are careful never to use humor to avoid hard conversations. Humor defuses tension and conflict, but if we take things too far, jokes turn to sarcasm. At least in our marriage, we've found that sarcasm does not build intimacy. Good-hearted humor does.

We do not have control over every trial of life, but we have plenty of input in finding joy *in* our trials. A couple either allows what life throws at them to bring them down or they maintain a sense of humor in the midst of it.

It is time to get serious about laughing together.

Humor helps us lighten up and not take ourselves so seriously. In other words, I can make fun of what I'm wearing or my own messy hair, but I don't do that to my wife. Part of our shared sense of humor is that Amy defends me when I'm using self-deprecating humor. It's odd when your spouse defends you to yourself, but it makes for some lighthearted, honoring moments in our marriage.

When is the last time you laughed together? How often do you try to make each other laugh? If it has been a while and your attempts are sparse, it is time to get serious about laughing together. Laugh at yourself today and invite your spouse to join in.

Let's TALK about It

Discuss the following questions together, today or throughout the week.

- Do we laugh together every day?
- If our family and friends were to describe the amount of levity in our marriage, what would they say?

- What does our shared sense of humor look like? Examples?

Let's DO Something about It

Are you ready to laugh, lighten up, cut loose, and enjoy life together?

- Make it a goal to bring a smile to your spouse's face every day this week.
- Share with your spouse something embarrassing that you said or did recently.
- Practice a joke on the way home and deliver it over dinner. It might not get a belly laugh, but more often than not, it will get a smile that says, "Thank you for the attempt."
- Print off a page of dad jokes from the internet and go back and forth at dinner tonight reading from the page. The goal is to keep a straight face. Try not to laugh, and you will discover that the restraint brings an extra layer of humor.

Let's PRAY about It

Prioritizing prayer will bring you closer together and pave the way for God to work in your life and relationship. Use the following prayer as a jumping-off point.

Father, thank you for creating laughter. Help us take you very seriously, but ourselves not so much. We want to bring more joy to each other in appropriate and fulfilling ways. Thank you for the lighter side of life. We want to honor you as we step into the appointed time to laugh. In Jesus' name. Amen.

Week 3

THE BENEFITS OF LAUGHTER

A time to weep and a time to laugh,
a time to mourn and a time to dance.

Ecclesiastes 3:4

Last week, we looked at our shared sense of humor and the joy it brings to marriage. This week, we turn to the benefits of laughter that keep the flames of humor stoked.

In Ecclesiastes 3:1, Solomon says, "There is a time for everything, and a season for every activity under the heavens." We do not choose the appointed times God has for us, but we do choose how we respond in those appointed times. Some seasons call for weeping and mourning, while others call for laughing and dancing.

A few times a year, I have the opportunity to speak at events to help couples laugh together. We call them Date Night Comedy events. After one such event recently, a precious senior lady hugged me without saying a word. It was an extended, emotional embrace that said a lot. She tried to speak but could not get the words out.

I asked, "Are you okay?" Usually, the only tears at Date Night Comedy are from laughing so hard you cry. But these tears were different.

It turned out that this sweet lady had lost her husband to COVID-19 the year before. Her brother and sister-in-law had invited her to join them for this night of relationship and marriage comedy. They believed she needed it. They were right.

"At first," she told me, "I could not for the life of me figure out why a widow needed a date night. I was not in the mood for laughter until I got here. Tonight brought back so many good memories. I laughed thinking of my husband's crazy antics. He would have loved tonight. He loved to laugh. I miss his humor."

Then *I* started crying. Even though, to paraphrase Tom Hanks's character in *A League of Their Own*, "There's no crying in comedy."

God used her family, church, and laughter that night to help her heal. Mourning is a season, and I knew she would continue to mourn. But that night had helped her move toward a season of transition.

How God uses humor and laughter to minister to people never ceases to amaze me. Laughter is an expression of joy. God gifts it to us, and heaven is filled with it. It heals us, helps us through stressful seasons, makes us enjoyable to be around, and binds us together. Let's look at a few of these great benefits.

Laughter reduces stress and relieves tension. My three favorite things to hear after I share at a Date Night Comedy event are, "I haven't laughed that hard in a long time," "My face hurts," and "My side hurts."

After a date night in Rock Valley, Iowa, a sweet senior lady shared with me, "Pastor, I have a fourth item to add to your list."

"What's that?" I asked.

She said, "I think I peed a little."

Laughter makes you more relatable. Have you ever walked into a room filled with laughter and started laughing? Like a yawn, laughter is contagious. We gravitate toward laughter even when we did not hear the story or joke that led to it.

We enjoy the company of those who do not take themselves too seriously. For the sake of your marriage, lighten up, and watch your spouse lean in.

Laughter helps us work through difficult conversations and uncomfortable subjects. Couples who use laughter to manage stress and work through difficult conversations not only experience higher levels of marital satisfaction but also stay together longer.

The key here is timing. After something happens that you perceive as funny, give it a little time before you make the joke. Husband, your wife is your greatest asset in figuring out timing. She will let you know when the time is right or when the joke is too soon.

If your marriage has been in a dry season for a while, invite laughter into your life. Let yourself go. Stop taking yourself so seriously. Shake your head at yourself and get the laughter started today.

Let's TALK about It

Discuss the following questions together, today or throughout the week.

- On scale of one to ten (with one being almost non-existent and ten being a lot), how often do we laugh?
- When was the last time you lost your breath or wore yourself out from laughing?
- What is the funniest thing I have ever said or done?
- How do you feel about our marriage when we laugh together?

Let's DO Something about It

Humor and laughter come naturally to some but not all. That's okay. Your mind can tell the difference between fake and real laughter, but your body cannot. That means all of us can experience the healing, stress-relieving benefits of laughter.

With no jokes or funny stories to lead out, which one of you will go first with the fake laugh? Look at your spouse and give your best fake laugh. Of course, it feels awkward. Don't give up too soon. Keep it going until you see your spouse smile. Better yet, keep it going until *you* genuinely chuckle.

Let's PRAY about It

Prioritizing prayer will bring you closer together and pave the way for God to work in your life and relationship. Use the following prayer as a jumping-off point.

Lord, you are our source of joy. Laughter is an expression of that joy. Thank you for giving us this great gift. We are grateful and hope to reap all these great benefits. Help us look for it and lean into it this week. Teach us to lighten up and enjoy life together. In Jesus' name. Amen.

BACKUP SINGERS

We rejoice and delight in you;
we will praise your love more than wine.

Song of Songs 1:4

The Song of Songs is the greatest duet of all time.

This eight-chapter, Old Testament duet is the love song of Solomon and the Shulammite woman. It starts with their young, budding love (chapters 1–2), moves to the wedding and honeymoon (chapters 3–4), and ends with building faithfulness and commitment into the marriage (chapters 5–8).

Throughout the lyrics, we hear from "the daughters of Jerusalem" as they sing backup. Every time they speak, they rejoice, delight in, and praise the love of Solomon and the Shulammite woman.

At Woodland Hills Family Church in Branson, Missouri, where I serve as pastor, we believe that every marriage is a duet in need of great backup singers. The quality of your marriage has a lot to do with the quality of the friends and family singing into it.

Every marriage needs voices that help with the harmony, voices that encourage the couple to prioritize each other. Some marriages drift because of the jaded, off-key voices singing over it. We determine the voices that back up our duet.

There are three considerations in choosing good backup singers.

First, they need to esteem marriage as highly valuable. If they see marriage or a spouse as a weight, hindrance, crutch, prison, or "the old ball and chain," invite them to surrender their microphones.

Second, choose backup singers who advocate for your marriage, not just for you. It's easy to pick sides when conflict arises, but you want someone who is for your future together. In-laws make great backup singers ... so long as they advocate for the *marriage,* not just for their child.

Third, a backup singer must set a good example. Just as I avoid financial advice from broke people swimming in debt, I ignore marriage advice from spouses who belittle each other in front of family and friends. Identify those couples who enjoy life together and hand them a microphone.

Identifying great backup singers is just the start. Be intentional with the relationship and invite them to speak into your marriage.

Amy and I have great backup singers in Jill and David Jones. Years ago, we agreed with them that we wanted to make our relationship more than a nice friendship in which we enjoyed occasional dinner dates together. God worked this out in our hearts and theirs. Our time with them is purposeful. They encourage and challenge us. We walk through difficult seasons together. We rejoice and mourn together. Our marriage is an open book to them.

You don't need a whole choir backing you up, but you do need a few good voices.

Never underestimate the power of a simple word of encouragement.

Do not overlook widows, widowers, and singles as backup singers. I meet regularly with a senior widow in our church who is a wellspring of encouragement for Amy and me. Her husband passed away thirty years ago. In fact, we never even met her husband, but the stories of their marriage minister deeply to us.

By the way, you need to be a great backup singer too. You have a lot to say about the quality of the marriages around you. There are couples in your life who need you to rejoice and delight in them. Never underestimate the power of a simple word of encouragement. Many marriages around you are starving to have life-giving words spoken over them.

Let's TALK about It

Discuss the following questions together, today or throughout the week.

- Who is someone who encourages our marriage on a regular basis?
- Are there any jaded, off-key voices that harmed our marriage in the past?
- Who is a couple that needs some backup singing from us?
- How can we best encourage them?

Let's DO Something about It

On one sheet of paper, write down the names of those speaking into your marriage at this time (e.g., coworkers, family members, church members, neighbors, friends, social media influencers, etc.).

Make your list together. Next to each person or couple on the list, write who needs to be muted, turned down, or turned up. (Muting someone doesn't necessarily mean you are cutting them out of your marriage or life. It simply means you are not allowing them to be an influence over you.) Those you choose to turn up are your backup singers.

Let them know of your decision. It will change your time with them for the better. It adds intentionality to your friendship.

Let's PRAY about It

Prioritizing prayer will bring you closer together and pave the way for God to work in your life and relationship. Use the following prayer as a jumping-off point.

Father, as you bless our marriage, we bless the marriages around us. We thank you for _____ (insert names of backup singers) _____. They are a great support to us. Bless their marriage and home. Remove distractions and give them conviction to stand together against the devil's evil schemes. Keep their path far from drift. And we pray for _____ (insert names of a couple you want to encourage) _____. Give us the words to say and the right time to say them. We want to be a blessing to their marriage. In Jesus' name. Amen.

FOOD AND FRIENDS

*Go, eat your food with gladness, and drink your wine with a
joyful heart, for God has already approved what you do.*

Ecclesiastes 9:7

The word *restaurant* comes from the French word meaning "to restore."
A good meal restores us physically, emotionally, relationally, and spiri-
tually. It is more than fuel for our bodies—it is also refreshment for
our souls and relationships.

Dan Cathy, CEO of Chick-fil-A, once told me, "A good meal
should restore you 30 percent in the stomach and 70 percent in the
heart. Unless of course you're a teenager, then we flip that."

Amy and I have wonderful memories of gatherings around the
table with family and friends, filled with life-changing conversations
and friendships forged in mealtimes. Some of the meals were simple,
while others were multicourse dining experiences.

The Bible has much to say about food and the central role it plays in
our relationship with God and others. The first-century believers "ate
together with glad and sincere hearts" (Acts 2:46). When Jesus told the
story of the prodigal son returning home to his father, the celebration
centered around a feast (see Luke 15:11–32). Jesus performed his first
miracle at a wedding, turning water into wine (see John 2:1–11).

We spend too much time asking each other, "What do you want to eat?" A better question would be "Who do we want to eat with, and why?" The who and why is far more important than the what.

We receive food and drink around the table with thanksgiving. "So, whether you eat or drink, or whatever you do, do all to the glory of God" (1 Cor. 10:31 ESV). "For everything created by God is good, and nothing is to be rejected if it is received with thanksgiving, for it is made holy by the word of God and prayer" (1 Tim. 4:4–5 ESV).

Most believers I know pray before mealtime. We thank God for our food, but do we take the time to thank him for the people gathered around the table?

Amy and I love hosting meals at our home. She is the expert on side dishes, and I am the novice on the Big Green Egg (charcoal grill). Over the years, we've picked up some helpful tips for increasing the joy we share with friends around our dinner table. I hope these ideas remove intimidation or hesitation in hosting friends and family and bring greater purpose to mealtime.

> **Be prepared.** In the days leading up to a hosted dinner, clean, remove clutter, and set the table. The more you can do days before the dinner, the more relaxed you'll be when your guests arrive.

> **Be present.** Remove distractions and technology. Give everyone at the table time to talk. Try to guide the conversation so everyone participates.

> **Be spontaneous.** Have some conversation starters in your back pocket, but home in on a story or struggle that presents itself during the meal. Tune in to the

emotions of your guests. Ask great questions. Do not hijack every conversation and make it about you or your agenda. Make it all about your guests.

Share Christ. We want Christ at the center of our marriage, home, and table. Consider ending the evening with prayer. Jesus said, "'I am the bread of life; whoever comes to me shall not hunger, and whoever believes in me shall never thirst'" (John 6:35 ESV). "Taste and see that the LORD is good" (Ps. 34:8).

Amy wants people at the end of a meal to think to themselves, *I matter to God, and I matter to them.* That is the heart of hospitality.

Let your marriage be a blessing to those who gather around your table. I believe God's favor is on us as we eat and drink with gladness and a joyful heart!

Let's TALK about It

Discuss the following questions together, today or throughout the week.

- What is your favorite meal?
- What is your favorite eating-out experience?
- What is your least favorite eating-out experience?
- With whom do we enjoying sharing meals the most?
- Is there any part of hosting a dinner party that intimidates you?
- Does anyone come to mind whom you would like to invite over for a meal this week?

Let's DO Something about It

Plan a double date with friends. It can be a meal out or at home. Choose your couple and the date and time. Here are ten conversation starters to get the talking going. Write them out and place them in your purse or back pocket, or take a picture of them to have handy.

- How did you two meet?
- How long did you date before you got married?
- Tell us about your wedding.
- Where did you go on your honeymoon?
- Tell us about your first home. What did you love about it?
- How many jobs have you had during your marriage?
- What was your worst job?
- What was your favorite job?
- What is your best childhood memory?
- Share with us the toughest season of your marriage. What did you learn from that season?

Let's PRAY about It

Consider the following prayer over your next meal.

Father, we thank you for the nourishment before us. You gave us the breath and strength to work for it, and you ultimately provide it. We receive it with thanksgiving. Thank you for _____ (list those gathered around the table) _____. Give them peace of heart and mind. Restore them in our time together. We pray this in the authority of the name of Jesus. Amen.

Week 6

YOUR MARRIAGE
ON DISPLAY

*But in your hearts revere Christ as Lord. Always be prepared to
give an answer to everyone who asks you to give the reason for the
hope that you have. But do this with gentleness and respect.*

1 Peter 3:15

Copenhagen, Denmark, is breathtaking. We vacationed there once.
From the brightly painted buildings lined up in a row to the warm
hospitality of the locals, our family soaked up every sight in this city.
We were there only one day, but the memory of those twenty-four
hours is happily seared into our hearts and minds.

It was the end of our family vacation, and I was starving after
three hours of walking. The iconic New Haven strip was our planned
destination for a quick bite. It turned out, though, that the only place
open was an Irish pub. I escorted my family in. Fish-and-chips were
not on my agenda, but the Lord walked us into that bar for a reason.

The pub was empty. Every table was open except one. A lady in
her late fifties sat with four empty Corona beer bottles in front of her.
It was not quite noon. She smiled and waved as though she were the
hostess. After we seated ourselves, she stepped outside for a smoke.

She returned a bit later and walked back to her table holding another Corona.

Tired but grateful for a place to sit down, we shared stories about our trip. Several of the stories brought big laughs, and we howled several times. Shortly after we ordered, the lady approached our table.

"I've been listening to your family," she said in a thick Irish accent. She pointed to our children and looked at Mary. "These two little [bleepers] are going to leave you one day. And you know what? You need to tell them to [bleep] off." She loved the F-word.

My kids sat stunned.

"Do you have a good marriage?" the woman asked.

"Well," I answered, "you're catching us at the end of a long family vacation, so we're tired. But yes, we have a great marriage."

She was caught off guard by my answer and launched back into, "You need a strong marriage, because these little [bleepers] right here are going to run off on you one day and you will be left with nothing!"

She talked to us for about ten minutes and then walked back to the bar.

"Wow," my kids said. "What was *that?*"

About a minute later, the woman approached our table with four Corona beers. "Can I buy your family a beer?"

"That is very kind of you, ma'am," I said, "but we're good."

I thought for sure the conversation was over, but we were just getting started. I prayed, "Okay, Lord, I know this is from you."

Amy asked the lady to share her story. It didn't take long to hear the hurt and to feel her pain. This sweet lady's mom had died three months earlier. She'd left her husband about a month after that, along with her business of thirty years. She'd traveled around Europe wearing her mom's coat because she'd promised her mom this trip years earlier but had been unable to fulfill it until now.

"I have nothing," she said at the end, weeping. "I've lost it all."

Amy asked her, "Do you believe you were created for a purpose? Do you believe there is something greater for you on this earth?"

She pointed at the two of us. "Well, you two have each other. But how do you know he won't leave you?"

"Yeah, we've got each other—that's true," I said. "But we've got something greater than each other." I gestured to Amy. "I love this woman. We enjoy life together. But she is not my source of life. One day, one of us will die. I know you left your husband, but there are a lot of ways to leave a spouse. Sometimes, that leaving is in death. But, ma'am, Jesus must be your source of life. Not your mom, not your sons, not your business, and not your husband. Jesus is your true and only source of life."

Amy and I took a few minutes to unpack the gospel for her.

She did not pray to receive Christ, but she was open. She told us that Amsterdam was her next stop. We shared with her the name of a church she could visit while there. She wrote it down in her journal. With that, she hugged Amy and our daughter goodbye.

The memory of that precious Irish woman sticks with us to this day. We talk about her often and wonder how she is doing. Is the moral of the story that Christians should spend more time in bars? Maybe. We miss so many opportunities like this when we hang out with people who look, think, believe, and act like us.

Amy tells me that my voice carries. My booming laugh turns heads in public. We often get a glance from neighboring tables in restaurants when I get on a roll. This Irish pub was no exception. Laughter introduced us to a precious woman and into a meaningful conversation. With gentleness and respect, we shared the name of Jesus. He is the reason for our hope. He is our source of life. We must always be ready to share his good name. He is our greater joy.

Let's TALK about It

Discuss the following questions together, today or throughout the week.

- When others engage us as a couple, do we make the most of the opportunities to share with them the source of our joy?
- Is there an individual or couple we need to spend more time with, keeping focused on our intention of sharing our faith with them?
- What are some fears that keep us from sharing Christ with family and friends?

Let's DO Something about It

Plan a dinner, gathering, or coffee date with someone you know is far from God.

- Start by asking them to share their story with you.
- Ask questions about their story.
- When the time feels right, share your testimony with them.
- Invite them to church.
- Tell them you love them, and ask if you can pray for them.
- Ask if there is anything specific you can help with or pray for.
- Ask if they would like to have a relationship with Jesus.
- If yes, invite them to pray with you.

Continue to pour into and encourage this person in the coming weeks, months, and years. Whether they desire a relationship with Christ or not, you have the opportunity to show them the love of Christ through your actions.

Let's PRAY about It

Fill in the blanks with the names of loved ones who need Jesus.

Father, right now we pray for _____(insert the names of lost family members, friends, or coworkers)____ and their salvation. Your word says that our love for each other shows the world that we are your followers. Let our love and light shine bright. Lead us into conversations that lead people to you and your Son, Jesus. With gentleness and respect, keep us on our toes with answers for the hope we have in you. Give us the words to say and the opportunity to say them. We love you and thank you for the opportunity to share your love. In Jesus' name. Amen.

AVOIDING MARITAL DRIFT

Catch for us the foxes,
the little foxes
that ruin the vineyards,
our vineyards that are in bloom.

Song of Songs 2:15

King Solomon described marriage as a vineyard. With care, hard work, sun, rain, and time, a vineyard produces grapes, which can be used to produce wine.

Solomon points out in this word picture that foxes sneak into the vineyard, nip the buds off the vines, and prevent the blooms that produce grapes. A few foxes can destroy an entire vineyard. Caring for a vineyard (or a marriage) requires us to chase off that which is destructive.

A fox is anything you allow into your marriage that could destroy your joy together. And it is often the little foxes that do the most damage. Big-ticket problems bring down marriages, yes. But it's the little problems we ignore and refuse to talk about that nip away at our joy in marriage.

Little foxes are the leading cause of marital drift. The longer the drift, the greater the distance between you and your spouse. Close the gap by identifying where you are currently in terms of drift and by deciding to pursue greater joy together.

Here are five signs of marital drift and the decisions you need to make to pursue greater joy.

When your marriage drifts, you'll find yourself blaming your spouse. Blame drains the marriage of life and energy. When you blame your spouse as the source of all your problems, you automatically set your spouse up to be the solution. Blame ends when you take 100 percent personal responsibility for your heart, emotions, words, and actions.

When your marriage drifts, you'll close your heart. Blame left unchecked turns to anger. A closed heart is filled with unresolved anger. Not to be confused with boundaries or a guarded heart, a closed heart is shut down and unwilling to let others in. Bitterness, resentment, and unresolved anger keep a heart on lockdown. Unresolved anger is like drinking poison but expecting your *spouse* to get sick. Anger can be buried, but it's always buried alive. It will resurface at other times and in other relationships.

Forgiveness is the decision to let your spouse off the hook. Just as your spouse is not your source of life, your spouse is not your source of forgiveness. Jesus is your source of forgiveness. "Be kind and compassionate to one another, forgiving each other, just as in Christ God forgave you" (Eph. 4:32). Forgive your spouse as God forgave you.

Unresolved anger is like drinking poison but expecting your *spouse* to get sick.

When your marriage drifts, you isolate from others. The longer your heart stays closed, the further you remove yourself from healthy voices. An unchecked, closed heart leads you to believe "No one understands what I am going through." That is not true. There are plenty of people in your life who have walked through difficult seasons. This is not the time to avoid them. Lean into them. "Listen to advice and accept instruction, that you may gain wisdom in the future" (Prov. 19:20 ESV).

When your marriage drifts, you doubt your future. You question the future of your life and marriage. You fall for the lies the world feeds you. If you find yourself doubting the future of your marriage, invite a trusted friend to lunch. Make sure the friend honors you and your marriage. Share your doubts and request the truth from them. Receive their counsel.

When your marriage drifts, you explore other options. Blame, resentment, isolation, and doubt bring us to the end. At this point, you search for someone or something else to make you happy. The most important decision you can make at this point to save your marriage is something I heard Dr. Scott Stanley say years ago: "Make the choice to give up all other choices." Burn the bridges.

A television commercial years ago quoted Newton's law of inertia: "A body in motion stays in motion. A body at rest stays at rest." Amy and I remember that first law of physics, but we have completely forgotten what the commercial was selling. Failed marketing aside, we quote that little line often.

A marriage in motion stays in motion. A marriage in drift stays in drift. You must choose to move forward in your marriage. Chase the foxes away. Personal responsibility, forgiveness, trusted voices, and commitment bring greater joy to your marriage.

Let's TALK about It

Discuss the following questions together, today or throughout the week.

- What are some of the little foxes we chased off early in our marriage?
- Are any little foxes sneaking around our marriage at the present time?
- When has drift caught us off guard?
- Which of the five signs of drift challenged our joy the most?

Let's DO Something about It

Take a look at the simple chart below representing the progression of drift. Make a mark on the chart where you think your marriage might be now. If you are not in drift, skip to the decisions and commitments section below the chart.

Blame ▸ Closed heart ▸ Isolation ▸ Doubt ▸ Exploring Options

Below, place your initials next to each decision and commitment that you agree will keep you out of drift.

_____ _____ I will not blame you for my thoughts, feelings, words, or actions.

_____ _____ I take personal responsibility for my thoughts, feelings, words, and actions.

_____ _____ I will not harbor resentment or bitterness toward you.

_____ _____ I will avoid the jaded voices in my life that lead me away from you and lean into trusted voices.

_____ _____ I make the choice to give up all other choices.

Let's PRAY about It

Prioritizing prayer will bring you closer together and pave the way for God to work in your life and relationship. Use the following prayer as a jumping-off point.

Lord, faith drift is every bit as real as marital drift. If we are not careful, we drift in our relationship with you. We commit to the decisions and spiritual disciplines that lead to enjoying life with you. Give us renewed passion for your Word, time with you in prayer, and gathering with believers. When we drift, we ask the Holy Spirit to call us by name and get us back on track. We thank you for the opportunity to be in right relationship with you. In Jesus' name. Amen.

THE PRINCESS IS NOW A QUEEN

For this reason a man shall leave his father and his mother,
and be joined to his wife; and they shall become one flesh.

Genesis 2:24 NASB

The bond between a husband and wife is to be stronger than the one between a parent and child. Your children will not be with you forever, but your marriage union lasts until the Lord returns or calls one of you home. Remind your children often that they are a welcome addition to your home but not the center of it.

For years, I have taught my kids a lesson from Genesis 2:24. I have them say, "I will not be with Mom and Dad forever, so I should plan accordingly."

Just for fun, I sometimes tell them, "Your mom and I have big plans for after you leave home." We are enjoying our marriage while parenting, and we plan on having great joy in the empty nest.

At my marriage conferences and date-night events for the past fifteen years, I have shared the story of my daughter, Corynn Mae, taking over the house when she was five.

I told her, "There is only one queen in this house, and you are not her."

She glared at me with eyes that said, *We will see about that.*

She told my wife, "There is room enough in this house for two queens."

When I heard that, I sat her down at the breakfast bar. "You are not the queen of this house," I said, "but you are my princess. One day, I'll walk you down the aisle to become another man's queen. From this day until that day, as you watch me with your mom, I want to show you every day how a queen should be treated."

On May 31, 2022, I walked my daughter down the aisle to become Caden Hazell's wife. She is now a queen.

Her wedding exceeded all our expectations. Corynn wanted a simple backyard garden wedding. We delivered on everything but the simple. It was elegant and radiant. I walked her down our backyard and our son, Carson, asked, "Who gives this woman to be married to this man?" After saying that her mother and I did, I stepped to the front to officiate.

You might be thinking to yourself, *How did you hold it together?* I did not. The video of the ceremony captured my sniffle every five seconds for thirty straight minutes. The microphone the videographer used was way too sensitive. My daughter calls the sniffles "presh." That is her term for *precious.*

For Corynn and Caden to thrive in marriage, they must leave their parents' homes physically, relationally, emotionally, and financially. Leaving home physically is easy to grasp. Leaving home relationally and emotionally is a bit more difficult.

Corynn is still my daughter, but our relationship changed that day. Now when she has great news to share, I am no longer her first phone call. When she needs to process through a big decision, Dad is not the first one she turns to for advice. But I definitely want to be her second call. Or third, after her mom. Top three, anyway.

We had two simple rules with the queen in our house: No one interrupts the queen when she speaks. No one runs ahead of the queen. The only way this latter rule could be violated was to open a door for the queen. I am grateful that my son-in-law treats Corynn Mae like a queen. I rejoice in their love and marriage.

Prioritizing my marriage to Amy was a big part of my parenting plan. Corynn observed in our home how to prioritize her marriage to Caden. Enjoying life together and expressing your joy in the home is a great gift for you and your children.

Let's TALK about It

Discuss the following questions together, today or throughout the week.

- What are some practical ways we can begin making this less of a kid-centered home?
- Is there anything about our calendar, schedule, or budget that needs to be realigned to prioritize our marriage in the home?
- We know that children feel more secure in the home when Mom and Dad are thriving in marriage. What are a few ways our kids feel safe because of our relationship?

Let's DO Something about It

Once you begin making decisions that prioritize your marriage in the home, have a conversation with your children. Here are a few talking points to share with them:

1. We love you.
2. You're a welcome addition to our home.

3. You won't be with us forever.

4. One day, you'll leave our home, and we want you
to be ready for the responsibility of relationships
and work.

5. Mom is the queen.

Let's PRAY about It

Prioritizing prayer will bring you closer together and pave the way for God to work in your life and relationship. Use the following prayer as a jumping-off point.

Jesus, make us one. With you at the center of our marriage, we want to prioritize our relationship in the home. May our kids see a mom and dad who carve out time for each other each day. We want our parenting to be an overflow of our marriage. Even now, we pray for the marriages of our children. Let our words and actions toward each other encourage their future marriages. Thank you for the gift of marriage, and for the opportunity to set an example of a Christ-centered marriage for our children. We love you, and it is in the name of Jesus we pray. Amen.

FIRST COMES LOVE, THEN COMES THE IN-LAWS

*So they are no longer two, but one flesh. Therefore what
God has joined together, let no one separate.*

Matthew 19:6

Matthew 19:6 begins with Jesus referring back to the idea of "one flesh" found in Genesis 2:24. A thriving marriage requires that we leave home and cleave to (connect with) our spouse.

Jesus adds, "let no one separate." As a new in-law, I do not want to be one who separates what God brought together in my daughter and son-in-law. I have a part to play in Corynn leaving home well and forming a deep bond with her new husband.

You may have heard the expression "You marry the family." That is not true. Corynn and Caden exchanged vows with each other, not with me. Your marriage is a covenant relationship with your spouse, not your parents.

Boundaries are the key to healthy relationships between you, your spouse, and your parents. They must be established, communicated, and honored. Here are a few boundaries we find helpful in our relationship with our parents and adult children.

Prioritize your spouse over your parents. The groom's mother approached me at a wedding years ago and said, "How dare you tell my son to stop loving his mother!" I had never told him that. What I *had* said to the young man was "Stop calling your mom multiple times a day. Give that time to your new wife. After a good day or a bad day, your mom is not to be your first phone call."

Prioritizing your spouse doesn't negate the love you have for your mom or dad, but it does change the frequency of phone calls and amount of time spent together.

Never negatively compare your spouse to a parent. Never compare your wife's meatloaf to your mom's. How your dad maintained the car does not need to be brought up in the conversation with your husband. Forge a new path together.

Have you ever visited your in-laws' house and heard them say something that reminds you of your spouse? That can be fun, but it does not need to be brought up in conflict. "You're reacting just like your mother" or "You sound like your father" are statements that will stoke the flames of conflict.

Do not allow your parents to make decisions for your marriage. This one gets a lot of couples in trouble. How you celebrate holidays and take vacations is up to you and your spouse, not your parents. If you want to be home and wake up in your house on Christmas Day, go for it. You are adults now. You do not need to call home and ask permission to make decisions.

Do not take personal responsibility for a parent's feelings, words, and actions. When you start making your own decisions, some people may get frustrated with you. Some people's feelings may get hurt. You are 100 percent responsible for your feelings, words, and actions. Your spouse is 100 percent responsible for their feelings, words, and actions. Your parent is 100 percent responsible for their feelings, words, and actions. By no means do we try to hurt a loved one's feelings, but they will get hurt, nonetheless. We are gentle and kind in our approach, but we need to let others tend to their own emotions.

Stop obeying—but never stop honoring—your parents. Caring leads to honor. The Bible calls me to honor and care for my parents until the Lord calls them home (Eph. 6:2). Esteem your parents as highly valuable. When you communicate a decision you know will upset them, lead out with your love for them. Let them know how much they mean to you.

When boundaries do not exist, are unclear, or are violated, the marriage suffers and the family is enmeshed. I love what my friend Jim Burns says to parents of adult children: "Keep your mouth shut and the welcome mat out." That pretty much sums up the boundaries I need to have in one simple statement. These boundaries help me to have a great relationship with my adult children.

Let's TALK about It

Discuss the following questions together, today or throughout the week.

- Of the five boundaries mentioned, which one is the hardest to establish and communicate with family?
- Are there any boundaries we need to do a better job of communicating with our parents?
- What are some practical ways to show our parents honor when communicating decisions we know will frustrate them or hurt their feelings?

Let's DO Something about It

1. Make a list of your current boundaries.
2. Add to the list any that are missing.
3. If any have not been communicated, talk through the necessary conversation with your parents.
4. If your boundaries are settled and communicated but violated, plan a sit-down with your parents to work through any misunderstandings. Proceed with care, caution, and humility.

Let's PRAY about It

Prioritizing prayer will bring you closer together and pave the way for God to work in your life and relationship. Use the following prayer as a jumping-off point.

Father, you call us to honor our parents and care for them. We honor you by honoring them. We want the best for our parents and desire a good relationship with them. Give us strength to establish boundaries and the courage to communicate them clearly. Give us the words to say and the time and place to say them. Thank you for our parents. It is in the authority of the name of Jesus that we pray. Amen.

Week 10

SIDE BY SIDE

But for Adam no suitable helper was found.

Genesis 2:20

Do not overlook the beautiful symbolism at the start of a wedding. Dad and daughter walk down the aisle side by side. Dad then steps aside, and another man comes alongside his daughter.

I walked side by side with my daughter through her childhood and into her young adult years. When I gave her hand in marriage to Caden Hazell, I stepped aside. He is now her side-by-side companion through the grind of life.

My wife loves Chip and Joanna Gaines. Their show *Fixer Upper* inspired many major projects around our home. At times, Chip wore me out with his giddiness toward household projects. I do not share his enthusiasm.

Amy and I attest to the challenges that come with married couples working together. Chip and Joanna know similar struggles, but they work through them in such a fun way. Joanna dreams, designs, and plans. Chip demos, takes instructions, and builds. It is a beautiful, complementary relationship.

Sometimes, I come home from work and Amy says something like, "I think after dinner, we're going to get rid of this wall right here." That's when I want to slap Chip's face. The first time she suggested tearing down a wall, I googled a term that saved our marriage: *load bearing.*

"Amy, every wall in our home is load bearing," I said. "You can't touch one or else the whole house comes down."

In all seriousness, Chip and Joanna inspire me. They are a great example of two very different people working side by side on a common vision.

Genesis 2:18 begins, "The LORD God said, 'It is not good for the man to be alone.'" In other words, man is better off when someone is with him.

So God said, "I will make a helper suitable for him." The word *helper* implies that the man needs someone to come alongside him where he is lacking. The Hebrew word for "helper" in Genesis 2:18 is *ezer,* which means "one who helps." It refers to someone who comes alongside to offer assistance. In fact, it is the same word used in Psalms 33, 70, and 115 to refer to God. He is your helper in times of trouble, your helper in times of difficulty:

> We wait in hope for the LORD; he is our *help* and our shield. (Ps. 33:20)

> Hasten, O God, to save me; come quickly, LORD, to *help* me. (Ps. 70:1)

> All you Israelites, trust in the LORD—he is their *help* and shield. (Ps. 115:9)

> So the man gave names to all the livestock, the birds in the sky and all the wild animals. But for Adam no suitable helper was found. So the LORD God

> caused the man to fall into a deep sleep; and while he
> was sleeping, he took one of the man's ribs and then
> closed up the place with flesh. Then the LORD God
> made a woman from the rib he had taken out of the
> man, and he brought her to the man. (Gen. 2:20–22)

God did not take a bone from Adam's head, implying that the woman should rule over man. He did not take a bone out of Adam's foot, implying that the man should rule over the woman. He took a bone from Adam's *side*. Husband and wife walk side by side through both the garden and life together. Through every blessing, challenge, opportunity, and storm, they have each other.

God gave you a spouse to come alongside you and to give assistance. He did not give you a spouse as a replacement for himself. We get to be *helpers*. We offer love, honor, encouragement, and support to each other. You are the CEO of your life; your spouse is not. You are responsible to God alone for how you live your life.

While Adam was sleeping, God took out one of his ribs and closed up the place with flesh. Then God made a woman from the rib he had taken out of the man. Genesis 2:23 says, "The man said, 'This is now bone of my bones and flesh of my flesh; she shall be called 'woman,' for she was taken out of man.'" Adam now had a spiritual, emotional, and physical companion. God's plan for your marriage is for you to spend your lifetime helping and serving each other, side by side.

Let's TALK about It

Discuss the following questions together, today or throughout the week.

- On what projects or chores do we work well together?
- What makes us work well together?

- Can you think of a project or chore in which we recently both felt flustered the entire time? What was it?

Let's DO Something about It

Plan and execute a small project around the house this week. For example, it could be cleaning out a closet, painting a room, planting a flower bed, or rearranging the furniture in a room.

Start with a plan and work toward a common vision for the project.

- When will you do it?
- What is the budget?
- What will be your part in the project?

After completion, sit in the room or closet together and discuss the best and hardest parts of the project.

- What could have made the project a little easier?
- If you were to do it again, what would you do differently to remove frustration?

Let's PRAY about It

Prioritizing prayer will bring you closer together and pave the way for God to work in your life and relationship. Use the following prayer as a jumping-off point.

Lord, you brought Eve to Adam for the first wedding. You designed marriage for a husband and wife to walk side by side through the grind of life. We will celebrate and honor our differences as we walk together. We will

call out the good work the other is doing and ask for ways we can help.
Thank you for being our perfect helper. May we glorify you through our
marriage and service to each other. In Jesus' name. Amen.

Through every blessing,
challenge, opportunity, and
storm, they have each other.

Week 11

ENJOYING STUFF YOU HATE

*Do nothing out of selfish ambition or vain conceit. Rather,
in humility value others above yourselves, not looking to your
own interests but each of you to the interests of the others.*

Philippians 2:3–4

Is there a script in your head that sounds like Toby Keith's country lyric "I wanna talk about me (me, me, me, me). I wanna talk about me (me, me)"?* Marriage is a great opportunity to work on keeping the flesh crucified. A good marriage requires that we keep our selfishness in check.

The spouse obsessed with self tends to control, nag, correct, demand, and nitpick. In contrast, the spouse considerate of the other loves, serves, honors, and sacrifices. Great marriages have two spouses who find great satisfaction in doing stuff for each other—even stuff they would never enjoy doing on their own.

For Amy and me, this list includes but is not limited to shopping, fine dining, remodeling kitchens and baths, decluttering, showering, dressing up, buying new clothes, stopping to use the restrooms on long

---

* Toby Keith, vocalist, "I Wanna Talk About Me," by Bobby Braddock, released August 20, 2001, on *Pull My Chain*, DreamWorks.

trips, watching *Life Below Zero*, watching Hallmark movies, taking romantic walks around the neighborhood at a brisk pace, chilling in the family room before 8:00 p.m., waiting in the Target parking lot, visiting my family, and visiting her family.

One of my wife's love languages is decluttering. She has two criteria that arise when she is using that love language: First, if you have not used it in a while, you do not need it. Second, if it no longer brings you joy, pitch it.

Influenced by Marie Kondo on Netflix's *Tidying Up*, Amy asks each article of clothing in our closet, "Do you spark joy?" If the answer is no, it goes in the donate-or-discard pile.

I remember the first time I caught her talking to a sweater. "What in the world are you doing?" I asked.

With a grin from ear to ear, she said, "I am getting rid of everything that no longer brings me joy, and I would like you to join me."

I believe I speak on behalf of men worldwide when I say we do not need to ask our jeans, "Do you spark joy?" Nope. They're jeans—of course they spark joy. We ask only two questions: "Do they still fit?" and "Do they smell?" If they pass those two tests, we keep the jeans.

Where does my wife like to go after the closet? Straight to the garage. She grabs the garbage can on wheels and walks it around like a grocery cart looking for items to throw away.

She holds up one item at a time and asks, "Are you still using this?"

"Babe," I plead, "that's a hammer."

As she tosses it in the garbage can, I run into the house to warn the children. "Mom's coming with the trash can. If you want it, hide it."

I am not a hoarder, but I like to keep some of my stuff. Amy is a minimalist. Joy fills her soul when her family declutters without her requesting it. Less stuff to clean equals greater joy for her.

To treat my wife to a shot of joy, I fill my arms with random stuff and announce I am headed to the donation box at the thrift store. But that is not enough. She also wants me to declutter with a good attitude.

How do I know I have a good attitude? How do I know if I am walking in humility? The answer is simple. "Do everything without grumbling or arguing" (Phil. 2:14). Grumbling and arguing are telltale signs that I am thinking about me, myself, and I.

Grumbling is complaining under your breath. You say something just loud enough so she knows you are not happy but not loud enough that she knows exactly what you said. Years of marriage experience perfects this technique.

Humility walks into the room and says, "There you are," not "Here I am." Humility is not irritated by doing activities your spouse enjoys. Humility expects nothing in return. Humility does not huff, pout, whine, or complain when treated like a servant. "Humility is the fear of the LORD; its wages are riches and honor and life" (Prov. 22:4).

If Amy finds joy in it, I will join her in doing it, and I will bring a joyful attitude to the party.

Let's TALK about It

Discuss the following conversation starters and questions together, today or throughout the week.

- What is your favorite activity around the house that you know I hate?
- What is my favorite activity around the house that you hate?
- The last time we did said activity, I appreciated the way you _____.

- The last time we did said activity, my attitude was not good because _____.

Let's DO Something about It

Each of you pick an activity around the house that you know your spouse loves. They do not get to pick their activity. You picking the right one shows your love and enthusiasm for this activity.

Do this activity together. With a new and improved attitude, get after it. No complaining under your breath. Take some time at the completion of the activity to appreciate each other's attempt.

Let's PRAY about It

Prioritizing prayer will bring you closer together and pave the way for God to work in your life and relationship. Use the following prayer as a jumping-off point.

Father, teach us to empty ourselves as Jesus did. He did not consider equality with God something to be grasped or used to his own advantage; rather, he made himself nothing by taking the very nature of a servant. We want to serve like Jesus without grumbling or arguing. Give us the patience, humility, and consideration to serve each other without any expectation for something in return. It is in the power and authority of the name of Jesus that we pray. Amen.

PRAY LIKE JESUS

And when you pray, do not be like the hypocrites, for they love to pray standing in the synagogues and on the street corners to be seen by others. Truly I tell you, they have received their reward in full.

Matthew 6:5

Jesus is not impressed by public prayers prayed to impress others. He is not talking about public prayers that edify others and build up the body of Christ. He implores us to avoid making it a show and to keep it between us and our heavenly Father.

> But when you pray, go into your room, close the door and pray to your Father, who is unseen. Then your Father, who sees what is done in secret, will reward you. And when you pray, do not keep on babbling like pagans, for they think they will be heard because of their many words. Do not be like them, for your Father knows what you need before you ask him. (Matt. 6:6–8)

When I first started dating Amy, our college pastor warned me, "Ted, make sure that you two do not pray together right away." I was shocked and questioned his reasoning.

He said, "Prayer is the most intimate thing you will ever do as a couple." He believed praying together was as intimate as physical intimacy. It took me a long time to wrap my brain around that thought, but twenty-five years later, I appreciate his passion for prayer.

Scripture refers to marriage as a one-flesh love (see Gen. 2:24). When a man leaves his parents to cleave to his wife, a bond is formed that is stronger than any other relationship on earth. We often think of physical intimacy as the deepest expression of that love. But is it?

In the Song of Songs, chapter 4, the wife's body is pictured as a garden. She extends an intimate invitation to her husband to enter and taste its choice fruits. It is hard to imagine anything bringing a couple closer than that, yet the apostle Paul called believers to pray during mutually agreed-upon times of sexual abstinence (see 1 Cor. 7:5). Praying with your spouse forms the strongest of bonds.

When you pray together, your transparency and vulnerability with your heavenly Father increase the depth and richness of your marriage bond. Here are a couple of practical considerations as you discover greater joy in prayer.

Break routine. Don't let mealtime be the only time you pray together. Avoid ruts by praying at other times of the day. Most Christians are taught the importance of beginning the day with prayer. However, ending the day in prayer deserves equal priority. It is hard to go to bed disconnected or angry with each other when you know you will be praying right before falling asleep.

Be real. Don't fake it. Confess your sins to each other when you pray (see James 5:16). Quick, trite, or repetitive prayers do not reveal what is really going on in your heart. Wordsmith your prayers much as you would any other conversation. If you were to say the same thing over and over again to your spouse, your marriage would grow stale and shallow. The same is true of your prayers. Keep them fresh and take your time. Don't fill the room with lofty but empty words.

Before you fall asleep tonight, reach for your spouse's hand, pray, and offer a gentle kiss good night. Inviting your spouse into your personal conversation with the Lord will ignite your marriage as well as your relationship with God.

Let's TALK about It

Discuss the following questions together, today or throughout the week.

- Why do couples so easily fall into ruts with prayer?
- When are some good times in our day in which we could concentrate more on prayer?
- How can I pray for you now?

Let's DO Something about It

Pray together tonight before you go to sleep. Here are some of the things Amy and I pray about at night. Maybe they will help bring to mind new ways to pray for each other.

Rest
Confession and repentance
Lament and mourning
Peace of heart and mind
Wisdom in leading our children
Our work
Gratitude for our home
Thankfulness for the resources we have to do life
Parents and their well-being

Church family
Sick and hurting
Widows and widowers
Those in need of salvation

Let's PRAY about It

Prioritizing prayer will bring you closer together and pave the way for God to work in your life and relationship. Use the following prayer as a jumping-off point.

Father, reignite our prayer time with you. We seek to pray without ceasing with prayers of adoration, confession, thanksgiving, and requests. This is our time to talk to you and hear from you. We commit to praying more together outside of mealtime. Our relationship with you is our reward. Thank you for the opportunity to know and be known by you. We love you. In Jesus' name. Amen.

Week 13

THE MARRIAGE BED

Marriage should be honored by all, and
the marriage bed kept pure.

Hebrews 13:4

The seasons of life change you and your spouse. Our bodies change, energy fades, and bedtimes get earlier. Twenty-five years into marriage and at almost fifty years old, I relate to the words of country music legend Toby Keith, "I ain't as good as I once was, but I'm as good once as I ever was."* I promise, that is my last Toby Keith lyric in this devotional.

Sexual desire is emotionally and physically healthy. Physical intimacy begins with emotional communication, not sexual connection. For this reason, sex is a barometer of the marriage. You solve most sexual problems outside the bedroom.

Two becoming one is a literal, physical, naked expression of marriage, but it is so much more than that. To become one flesh in marriage, you cannot be a controlling, intimidating, harsh spouse by day and a gentle, tender, pleasure-giving lover at night. Honor your

---

* Toby Keith, vocalist, "As Good as I Once Was," by Toby Keith and Scott Emetic, released May 9, 2005, on *Honkytonk University*, DreamWorks Nashville.

marriage and keep the marriage bed pure by honoring your spouse both day and night.

Longing to be with your spouse sexually is a healthy response to your sexuality. Sex is for mutual enjoyment between a husband and wife. God wants you to be sexually intoxicated with your spouse (see Prov. 5:19). God does not want you to be sexually intoxicated with someone else's spouse (see vv. 15–16, 20).

The Song of Songs offers four keys to sexual exclusivity and enjoyment in the marriage bed.

First, be gentle. "Your breasts are like two fawns, like twin fawns of a gazelle that browse among the lilies" (Song 4:5). Fawns are skittish and delicate. You do not rush toward them, and you are never rough with them. Gentleness is the first step toward safety, both in the heart and in the marriage bed.

Second, pursue endurance. "Until the day breaks and the shadows flee, I will go to the mountain of myrrh and to the hill of incense" (Song 4:6). "Quickies" are good, but they can invalidate the wife's desire to orgasm. Think five-course meal, not fast food. Lovemaking is best done slowly and unrushed.

Third, provide safety. "You are altogether beautiful, my darling; there is no flaw in you" (Song 4:7). Physical insecurities are best resolved by a loving spouse within a healthy marriage. Never say a negative word about your spouse's body. Rather, speak constantly of its beauty.

Finally, increase frequency. "Eat, friends, and drink; drink your fill of love" (Song 5:1). Someone asked once through our church website, "How often should an Evangelical couple have sex?" We have no Scripture mandating the number of times per week, but the Song of Songs implies that often is better than seldom.

Sex is beautiful, wonderful, and powerful. When you give your body to your spouse, you become one in flesh. Sex is not meant to be used as a weapon or a reward but to be mutually enjoyed in a safe environment. The best sex of your life requires communication.

There will be more than a few moments in a marriage when it's not the optimal time for sex. It's okay to say, "Not right now," or "I need some time," but remember the scriptural guidance on this. The Bible instructs that a married couple should "not deprive each other [of sex] except perhaps by mutual consent and for a [limited] time" (1 Cor. 7:5). Sex should never be used to manipulate or control the person you love.

There is greater joy in the marriage bed when the couple accelerates spiritual, relational, and emotional intimacy. Be safe and gentle lovers who bring great pleasure to each other often.

Let's TALK about It

Start individually by placing a check mark next to the questions you feel safe discussing, each taking a turn. Then, together, discuss only those questions where you've both placed a check mark.

____ ____ How often, if ever, did you and your parents talk about sex?

____ ____ What kind of picture did your parents paint for you about sex?

____ ____ When and where did you first learn about sex?

____ ____ Is sex an embarrassing subject for you?

____ ____ Are there any questions about sex that you think are off limits for us to discuss?

____ ____ Give an example of an off-limits question.

____ ____ What parts of your body are you insecure about? What can I do to ease those insecurities?

____ ____ Do you like it when I undress in front of you? Should I slow it down?

____ ____ What would you change about our bedroom environment to spice it up?

____ ____ On a scale of one to ten, how satisfied are you with how often we have sex?

____ ____ I enjoy having sex ____ times per week or month.

____ ____ How often do you reach climax/orgasm when we have sex?

____ ____ Do we do well sharing the initiation?

____ ____ Do we offer grace to each other when one of us thinks, "Tonight's the night," and the other thinks, "Not tonight"? Do we ever show anger?

____ ____ On a scale of one to ten, how satisfied are you with our performance?

____ ____ What can we do to bring our sex life out of a rut?

____ ____ Can you give me two or three ideas for foreplay?

____ ____ What position is most comfortable for you?

____ ____ What can we do to create a more romantic atmosphere for lovemaking, such as candles, scents, or music?

____ ____ On a scale of one to ten, how satisfied are you with how long we spend making love?

Let's DO Something about It

There's nothing wrong with a scheduled night of romance, intimacy, and sexual pleasure. Mark a special night on the calendar this week and prepare your hearts, minds, bodies, and environment. Concentrate your thoughts toward the night on the days leading up to it. Consider candles, lotions, music, and dimmed lights. Set a generous amount of time. Enjoy the marriage bed together.

Let's PRAY about It

Prioritizing prayer will bring you closer together and pave the way for God to work in your life and relationship. Use the following prayer as a jumping-off point.

Father, make us one. We want our bedroom to be safe, free, and enjoyable. We will guard the marriage bed from anything the world would use to pervert it. Our eyes are for each other and no other. We honor our marriage with intimacy that honors you. In Jesus' name. Amen.

NO BIG DEAL

A person's wisdom yields patience;
it is to one's glory to overlook an offense.
Proverbs 19:11

Amy and I visited her home in Fremont, Nebraska, in December of 1996 to celebrate Christmas with her family. As newlyweds for all of two months, we had a lot to learn about our families and each other.

A couple of days after Christmas, the family decided in the morning to go to a 7:00 p.m. movie that night.

At about 6:45 that night, everyone was sitting in the family room with their shoes off.

"Did we decide to stay in tonight?" I asked. That was no big deal. I was actually okay with staying in for the night.

"No," Amy said, "we're going to a movie."

"How far away is the theater?"

"About ten minutes."

At this point, there was still no movement toward the door by any member of her family. No one had a coat on, and our shoes were in a pile by the door.

My mind raced with confusion. Purchasing tickets at the box office, picking out snacks, and finding our seats was a twenty-minute commitment, not even counting travel and parking time. But everyone was sitting comfortably in the house. No lie: while I processed all this, one member of the family went to the kitchen and got a snack.

Then my father-in-law stirred. "The first ten minutes of the movie are previews, and we can miss those."

What? I grew up in a home that taught, "If you're five minutes early to anything, you're late." Being on time and in my seat early is in my DNA. Besides, I love movie previews as much as the feature presentation.

Amy's family is not wrong for not needing to see the previews. For them, it felt like commercials, and who likes commercials?

A different way is not the wrong way. The inconsequential differences between you are just that—inconsequential. They are of no consequence. Keep that in mind. Learn to let minor frustrations go before they escalate. Find a way to have fun with them.

A different way is not the wrong way.

Do you want a term that will set you free in marriage? Say "NBD" (no big deal) the next time you spot one of the differences.

For example, toilet-paper-roll placement is an NBD moment. Over the top or down the back? NBD. What about toothpaste dispensing? The neatly rolled tube or the tube squeezed in the middle? NBD. Toilet seat up or down? NBD. Your wife using your razor to shave her legs? NBD. Thermostat setting? NBD.

Some couples treat everything as a VBD (very big deal). Turning every little thing into a big thing builds up stress like a volcano waiting to erupt. The eruptions are messy and destructive. There is a better way.

Most marriage experts encourage couples to discuss minor offenses as they occur. Do not sweep them under the rug—deal with them. That's valid, but Proverbs 19:11 says to overlook an offense. I'm not saying sweep it under the rug. I'm saying sweep it into a dustpan and take it out with the trash.

Amy has plenty of NBD moments with me. She's a master at letting things go and overlooking minor offenses.

She confessed recently to loading the dishwasher the "wrong way" so that I would do the dishes. She let that slip one night while I was reorganizing the dishwasher racks. Early in our marriage, dishwasher loading was an ongoing conversation and a constant source of frustration, as we each had different ideas about what was the "right way." Not anymore. Amy let it go and says, "No big deal."

Let's TALK about It

Discuss the following questions together, today or throughout the week.

- Name one thing I do that drives you crazy around the house.
- Name one thing you do that drives me crazy.
- In your opinion, what are some of the differences between "very big deal" and "no big deal" moments?
- What's the best and fastest way to turn a VBD into an NBD?

Let's DO Something about It

Take time this week to talk through your household chores. Some couples share duties around the house, while others divide and conquer. In the space below, make your list. This is a good time to discuss minor offenses that you overlook. Keep it light and friendly.

<table>
<tr><th>His Chores</th><th>Her Chores</th></tr>
<tr><td>_____</td><td>_____</td></tr>
<tr><td>_____</td><td>_____</td></tr>
<tr><td>_____</td><td>_____</td></tr>
<tr><td>_____</td><td>_____</td></tr>
<tr><td>_____</td><td>_____</td></tr>
<tr><td>_____</td><td>_____</td></tr>
<tr><td>_____</td><td>_____</td></tr>
</table>

Let's PRAY about It

Prioritizing prayer will bring you closer together and pave the way for God to work in your life and relationship. Use the following prayer as a jumping-off point.

Father, you have cast our sins as far as the east is from the west. Yet sometimes we hold the small things against each other. Give us eyes to see and ears to hear the value in our spouse. We don't want to be sidetracked by trivial and inconsequential issues. We will choose patience and keep no record of wrongs. That is love. We seek to glorify you in our words and actions toward one another. It is in the mighty name of Jesus we pray. Amen.

MAKING THE MOST OF THE TIME

Our days may come to seventy years,
or eighty, if our strength endures;
yet the best of them are but trouble and sorrow,
for they quickly pass, and we fly away.

Psalm 90:10

If I live to be eighty years old, I will have had 29,200 days here on earth. At the writing of this devotional, I have already lived 17,632 days. I am in the third quarter of the game. Perhaps you are in the fourth quarter. I know a few who are in overtime.

Time is funny and seems always to be fleeting. We say things like, "I wish we had more time," "Sorry, but we're out of time," "Where has the time gone?" "Time got away from us," and "Time sure flies." One way to make the most of time is to number our days. According to the Bible, this leads to wisdom: "Teach us to number our days, that we may gain a heart of wisdom" (Ps. 90:12).

Life is both short and uncertain. In light of these two truths, we ought to be "redeeming the time" (Eph. 5:16 KJV) rather than wasting it. Let's ponder these two biblical truths as we apply them to marriage.

First, Psalm 39:4–5 teaches us that *life is short*:

> Show me, LORD, my life's end
>> and the number of my days;
>> let me know how fleeting my life is.
> You have made my days a mere handbreadth;
>> the span of my years is as nothing before you.
> Everyone is but a breath,
>> even those who seem secure.

Second, Proverbs 27:1 reminds us that *life is uncertain*: "Do not boast about tomorrow, for you do not know what a day may bring."

Yes, life is short and uncertain, but the choice to be wise with your time is up to you. One thing I've noticed about people who live with purpose is that they're more intentional with how they spend their time. If I give all my time to work or to making a name for myself, my family suffers. I have never once in my life regretted time given to my wife and family.

Make time for people … because people matter most. When you regard the brevity of life head-on, what matters most hits you in the face. Do not wait to experience it. Know the truth and make better choices because of it.

Amy and I were recently on a flight that lost an engine during takeoff. The plane shuddered and made noises that even seasoned travelers among us had never heard. The flight attendants made eye contact with one another and appeared concerned. As I looked around the plane, every single person was on their phone. I saw no one checking stock prices or scrolling social media. They were all texting family and friends.

I sent a quick text to our children saying, "I love you all and I hope you have a great day." I know, kind of lame for a last text. When the end is near, the pressure is on.

The plane made an emergency landing, and everyone on board was safe. Sitting in the gate area waiting for a new plane, we talked to the other passengers about those "final moments." There was a sense of relief among all of us. It was a good jolt back to the reality that life is short and uncertain. When we thought our lives might be coming to an end, we made the most of those minutes on the plane.

Make time for people ...
because people matter most.

Be on the lookout for opportunities to serve your family this week. Keep your "head on a swivel," as the saying goes, for the family member who needs a word of encouragement. Walk into your kid's room with a "There you are" attitude, not a "Here I am!" one.

Do it today, because you're not promised tomorrow. For those of us who might tend to see opportunities and say, "Not today," we must hear the words of Proverbs 3:28: "Do not say to your neighbor, 'Come back tomorrow and I'll give it to you'—when you already have it with you."

Do it now. Say it now. Hug her now. Pray with him now. Leave the note now. Send the text now. Make the phone call now.

Let's TALK about It

Discuss the following questions together, today or throughout the week.

- How does the truth that life is short and uncertain change the way you live?

- Do you remember a time when you came face to face with the brevity of life (e.g., accident, funeral, etc.)?
- How did it affect your decisions moving forward?

Let's DO Something about It

Open your calculator on your phone.

Multiply your age by 365.

Subtract it from 29,200.

Enter the number here: _____.

Let that number sink in. If you live to be eighty, that's how many days you have left.

Discuss how you will make the most of your remaining days.

Let's PRAY about It

Prioritizing prayer will bring you closer together and pave the way for God to work in your life and relationship. Use the following prayer as a jumping-off point.

Father, teach us to number our days. We want our remaining days to count for you. Give us hearts of wisdom with planning for the future. We confess the times we have been arrogant with our plans. We submit all our plans to you. Direct our paths. Many are our plans, but you ultimately direct our steps. You are sovereign over our days. We will praise and glorify you for the rest of our days on earth. We thank you for the time you have given us, and for those people you have surrounded us with. In Jesus' name. Amen.

Week 16

THE DAILY DELAY

My beloved is to me a sachet of myrrh
resting between my breasts.
Song of Songs 1:13

In Solomon's day, a woman perfumed her body at night with a "sachet of myrrh." Much like the custom from generations past of a spice pouch in the dresser permeating the clothes, the sachet stayed with the Shulammite woman all night. This is a word picture for the thoughts she has of Solomon. She goes to sleep thinking about him, dreams about him, and wakes up with him on her mind. Remember those days and nights when you were dating and you couldn't stop thinking of each other?

In our first months of dating, I once fell asleep on a late-night phone call with Amy. She let me know the next day. We loved spending time together. When we were apart, we thought about each other nonstop.

Even as your thoughts get crowded out by other responsibilities, hopefully you are still refreshed when you and your spouse think about each other. I want the mention of my name to bring a smile to my wife's face.

More than twenty years ago, one of my mentors told me, "Ted, if you're going to thrive in ministry and marriage, you and Amy need to prioritize a daily delay, a weekly withdrawal, and an annual abandon." We heeded that advice and follow it to this day. We prioritize each other when we prioritize time together.

A *daily delay* is fifteen to twenty minutes a day of tech-free, kid-free, and distraction-free conversation. We talk about the house, budget, schedules, church, parenting, and upcoming trips. Sometimes, the conversation is serious and heavy, and other times it is more laid-back. We like to laugh and dream together, and our daily delay facilitates that.

Our good friends Greg and Erin Smalley taught us about "touch points" and how to incorporate them into daily life. Touch points are the moments throughout the day when we connect, depart, or cross paths. The simple gestures and words in those moments matter in the long run.

The "Good morning!" when we awake is a touch point. So is the "Goodbye!" as we head out for the day. The "Just checking in" phone calls throughout the day, the "Honey, I'm home" reconnection at the end of the workday, and the "Good night" as our heads hit the pillows are all touch points.

After a few years of marriage, touch points tend to get lost or filled by other things. For example, many of us reach for our phone first thing in the morning. If this is a rut in your marriage, commit to touch your spouse before you touch any device. If you've drifted away from kissing first thing upon arriving home at the end of the day or the end of your shift, get back to some nonsexual touching.

I talk to a lot of couples about their daily delays and most agree that the reconnection point at the end of the workday is not a great time to sit down for that fifteen-to-twenty-minute conversation. Each person needs to decompress for a few minutes, mow the lawn, play with the kids, or get dinner ready. No problem. Do not pressure yourself to get eye to eye with each other as soon as you walk through the door.

Quality time happens between you naturally early on in your relationship, but you must become intentional about it later. No one needs to tell a dating, engaged, or newlywed couple to spend more time together or to touch each other more often. It is like breathing, at first. When it fades, we need to become intentional with it. Get back to some of those good times you had early on and prioritize the daily delay.

Let's TALK about It

Discuss the following questions together, today or throughout the week.

- How long does it take each night for you to unwind from your day physically, emotionally, and relationally?
- What is your best time of day to sit down to be eyeball to eyeball and face to face? Early morning? Midday? After dinner? After the kids go to bed? (The best time for a daily delay will differ from couple to couple.)

Let's DO Something about It

Pick your time of day, and get the daily delay started. Try these conversation starters:

What was the hardest part of your day?
What was the best part of your day?
If I played hooky tomorrow, I would _____.
What made you feel the most productive at work today?

What was your biggest distraction?

Did you talk to anyone interesting today?

If you knew you couldn't fail, what would you wake
up tomorrow and do?

Let's PRAY about It

Prioritizing prayer will bring you closer together and pave the way for
God to work in your life and relationship. Use the following prayer as
a jumping-off point.

*Father, our daily time with you is the most important part of our day. Our
time with each other is important as well. Help us to remove distractions
and focus on you and one another. Time with you and each other will
be a priority from this day forward. Give us the capacity and desire to
prioritize this time. We love you. In Jesus' name. Amen.*

Week 17

THE WEEKLY WITHDRAWAL

Listen! My beloved!
Look! Here he comes,
leaping across the mountains,
bounding over the hills.
My beloved is like a gazelle or a young stag.
Look! There he stands behind our wall,
gazing through the windows,
peering through the lattice.
My beloved spoke and said to me,
"Arise, my darling,
my beautiful one, come with me."

Song of Songs 2:8–10

The weekly withdrawal is our date night. Every date communicates to our children, family, and friends, "Our marriage is important."

The daily delay is for keeping short accounts on the details of running our home, which protects our weekly withdrawal from logistical conversations. Nothing ruins a date night faster than turning it into a business meeting. Do not spoil your date night by talking about the budget or the kids' schedules. Save all that for the daily delay. However, there are times when your marriage is burdened by something heavy that requires more than the daily delay. Date night is a great time to work through conversations weighing on your heart.

Amy and I keep date night light and fun. We like to try new activities and restaurants. Since most of our evening walks are in our neighborhood, we sometimes drive to other neighborhoods for our walk on date night. We love looking at houses and landscaping and finding fresh ideas for our own.

One of the keys to great dating is anticipation. It initiates the plan and lets you enjoy it days before the actual date. That's what the Shulammite woman describes in this passage. Solomon comes to get her. His enthusiasm and excitement abound. He stands, gazes, and peers before inviting her to "come with me."

Spontaneous date nights are fun too, but planning a few days out gives anticipation some time to build. My wife loves to get on the restaurant's website days before to look over the menu. We discuss appetizers, entrées, and desserts. It is a fun way to whet our appetites.

Two common excuses for skipping date night are "We have kids" and "We don't have money." You do not need to spend a lot of money to spend a few hours alone each week. Walks, hikes, and sightseeing are free. Quick-service meals and window-shopping are cheap. For the pricier dates, make a plan in your family budget. It cracks me up when a spouse sips a venti Frappuccino from Starbucks while explaining to me that dating is too expensive.

For childcare concerns, lean into grandparents and family members. I look forward to the day when we will babysit our grandkids so our adult children and their spouses can go out on dates. We get two for the price of one by backup singing for their marriage and by spending time with our grandchildren. Also, you can take turns with friends watching your kids and you watching their kids in what I call the Great Date Night Exchange. Another option is to budget for childcare. Your marriage and children are worth it.

Every couple makes excuses and gets into ruts in dating. Break out of the old "dinner and a movie" rut and think of some dating adventures. Roller-skating, kayaking, spelunking, cooking classes, painting or ceramics classes, or a scenic drive might be the jump start your weekly withdrawal needs. Plan, anticipate, and enjoy quality time together.

Let's TALK about It

Discuss the following questions together, today or throughout the week.

- What time of day are we at our best as a couple? How might this inform the times we reserve for our daily delay and weekly withdrawal?
- What distractions do we need to remove to make the most of our time together?
- What should we do for a date night this week? Are we up for something new, fun, playful, or adventurous?
- If we had no budget or time constraints, where in the world would we like to go or what in the world would we like to do?
- Not only do we need to consider who speaks into our marriage, but we also need to be great backup singers for other couples. Who in our circle of influence needs some encouragement right now? Should we consider inviting them to join us for a double date next week?

Let's DO Something about It

This week, make an effort to schedule a weekly withdrawal. Remember, satisfaction in your marriage is a choice, not an automatic outcome. It's important to prioritize time together. If you need inspiration, below are a few activity ideas for date night.

- Find a sitter for the kids, grab some quick take-out, and eat together at the nearest park. In case of inclement weather, sit inside the restaurant or your car. The important thing is to create some alone time away from your responsibilities at home. Silence your cell phones and try to eliminate distractions.
- If you cannot afford a sitter, put the kids to bed and order a pizza. Light some candles and create a little ambiance. Or keep it low key and eat on the couch. But leave the TV off and put your cell phones away! Aim for at least one hour of uninterrupted time to just enjoy being together.
- Speed-date your spouse. Google a list of five to ten silly icebreaker questions and take turns answering them. Set aside your preconceptions and pretend you're getting to know each other all over again. Embrace the goofiness!

Let's PRAY about It

Prioritizing prayer will bring you closer together and pave the way for God to work in your life and relationship. Use the following prayer as a jumping-off point.

Father God, we acknowledge that you are the center of our marriage. As we carve out room in our busy schedules for quality time together this week and in the weeks to come, help us show grace to each other. We are grateful that you have brought us together and for all the ways you continue to work in our hearts, relationship, and family. Help us experience greater joy together as we seek you and prioritize our relationship. It is in the power of the name of Jesus that we pray. Amen.

THE ANNUAL ABANDON

Come, my beloved, let us go to the countryside,
let us spend the night in the villages.
Let us go early to the vineyards
to see if the vines have budded,
if their blossoms have opened,
and if the pomegranates are in bloom—
there I will give you my love.

Song of Songs 7:11–12

The daily delay is fifteen to twenty minutes at home of distraction-free conversation. The weekly withdrawal is a date away from home but still around town. The annual abandon requires luggage. Pack a suitcase and get out of town!

In Song of Songs 7:11–12, the Shulammite bride invites her busy, shepherd-king husband, Solomon, to get out of town. This invitation breaks routines and schedules in favor of some much-needed romance and intimacy. And just like the date night, planning and anticipation make this even better.

Amy and I love to schedule our annual abandon four to six months in advance. That gives us plenty of time to dream, discuss activities, and research a number of restaurant menus. The months leading up to the trip are almost as fun as the getaway itself. And then, like the couple who talks about dinner while eating lunch, we plan our next trip while on a trip.

Our past annual abandons have been to the mountains, vineyards, and the beach. Our all-time favorite abandon is New York City. We both love the diversity, sights, food, and entertainment of the Big Apple. Amy walks me until my feet fall off every time we visit, and I love it. We get twelve to fifteen miles' worth of steps in from sunrise to well after sunset. I need the mileage to justify the pizza and street pretzels.

Here are key factors Amy and I consider to make our annual abandon unforgettable:

First, we do not need to be gone for a week. Actually, our preferred time frame is two to four days. As foodies, a week of eating is too much. But with only three nights away, we tap out with zero regrets. Amy warns me on day three that a no-sugar diet awaits us at home.

Shorter trips are easier on the budget too. We stay in nicer hotels and eat better meals because the time is short.

Second, out of town does not have to mean a long way from home. Sometimes the closest big city works for us. This cuts down on the travel and saves money for eating and shopping.

Third, make best use of the time by including some work and marriage goals. Our friends the Stoevers and the Donyes are the best at this. They use their annual abandons to work through questions that deepen their relationship, and they plan for their family in the coming year. It is a reset time for them.

Finally, let's be honest: more than one annual abandon is more than possible. We prefer two shorter trips per year over one long one. The older we get, the more we love being home. Going on a trip is great, but we love the return just as much. Annual abandons make you appreciate home.

In the seventh chapter of Song of Songs, the Shulammite bride describes the countryside and vineyards in great detail. In the midst of the setting, she states her intention: "There I will give you my love." She plans to make love in the vineyard. How beautiful is that?

Free of distractions, work, and kids, the annual abandon gives us time to enjoy one another physically. No rushing. No quickies. Just husband and wife relaxed, unhurried, and fully connected.

Let's TALK about It

Discuss the following questions together, today or throughout the week.

- What's the best trip we have ever taken together? What made it so great?
- Where's our preferred go-to spot when it's just the two of us? Beach, mountains, forest, desert, resort, cruise, attraction, landmark, or city?
- If money and time were of no concern, where would we go and how long would we spend there?
- If we could have a redo on our honeymoon, where would we go?

Let's DO Something about It

Let's plan an annual abandon. It doesn't have to be our next one. We might want to plan one to take years from now. Remember, planning and anticipation are keys to greater joy together.

Where are we going? _____

What's the best time of year to visit this place? _____

How long will we stay? _____

What is the budget? _____

What dinner reservations do we need to make? _____

_____

What attractions will we visit? _____

_____

Who will watch the kids? _____

Let's PRAY about It

Prioritizing prayer will bring you closer together and pave the way for God to work in your life and relationship. Use the following prayer at the beginning of your planning session for the annual abandon:

Father, just as time alone with you grows our relationship with you, we want our marriage to have the same uninterrupted time. As we plan time away, we want to honor you as we honor each other by making the most of our time. Intimacy with you and each other is our goal. Unhurried time together is our plan. Thank you for the gift that is our marriage and the opportunity to be in intimate relationship with one another. In Jesus' name. Amen.

Week 19

TIME FOR WHAT MATTERS MOST

And he took the children in his arms, placed
his hands on them and blessed them.

Mark 10:16

In Jesus' day, women and children were second-class citizens. Childhood was an insignificant season of life. Little boys had greater value than little girls. Jesus turned all that upside down. His life and ministry valued all women and children. He made time for people, because people matter most.

In Mark 10:13 we read, "People were bringing little children to Jesus for him to place his hands on them, but the disciples rebuked them."

The disciples rebuked them because they did not esteem children. They did not see these children as highly valuable, created in God's image. Jesus quickly declared their worth in his eyes. The Bible says he was very angry with his disciples: "When Jesus saw this, he was indignant. He said to them, 'Let the little children come to me, and do not hinder them, for the kingdom of God belongs to such as these'" (Mark 10:14).

Amy and I want to value people and make time for them, just like Jesus did.

Our tasks at work, ministry at church, time around the table with friends, and visits with sick family members in the hospital are priorities for our family. As a pastor, a top priority for me is sermon preparation and delivery. I spend time on it because it is important, but it is not the most important part of my life. It does not define me.

One Sunday morning when our daughter was four, she escaped from her class at church. I was in the middle of a sermon when I saw her waving at me from the back of the auditorium. I waved back and gave her a wink. That did not suffice, and she took it as permission to come ask me a question right in the middle of the service.

As she walked down the center aisle, I got nervous. She walked right up onto the stage and asked me, "Have you seen Mom?"

Not only were we going to have a conversation, but the congregation would hear every word over my microphone. Corynn spoke to me as though no one else was there.

"Corynn," I said, "we are in the middle of the sermon, and I need you to go back to your class."

"Daddy, Mom said Emma could come over after church, and I want to see if Lucy can too."

With every eye in the room watching me, I got down on one knee and worked through our after-church social arrangements. Then I kissed Corynn goodbye, and she went back to her class.

At that moment, the impromptu sermon trumped my prepared sermon. Our worship pastor said it was the best sermon he had ever seen. All these years later, people still talk about that moment and its impact. When was the last time you set aside something very important for something even more important?

Interruptions such as these are defining moments for parents. You cannot schedule them, but you can embrace them when they happen. Patiently responding to an interruption communicates love and concern, and it also demonstrates how to care for and prioritize the ones you love. Interrupting a football game on TV, stopping the mower for a chat, closing a book while studying, and even pausing in the middle of a sermon shows our children that they matter to us.

Be on the lookout this week for at least one opportunity to pause an important task to give time to what matters most.

Let's TALK about It

Discuss the following questions together, today or throughout the week.

- When was the last time our children or grand-children interrupted us while we did something important?
- How did we respond to that interruption?
- Looking back, what could we have said or done differently?
- Do our children or grandchildren ever feel like a distraction in our home?
- Name a few tasks that you tend to overvalue. Name a few that I tend to overvalue.

Let's DO Something about It

When we treat those we love like an interruption, they do not feel valued. When we make time for them in the busyness of life, they feel valued.

Stop yourself this week in the middle of an important task to engage a family member in conversation. Beat them to the punch. Don't wait for them to approach you for your time. Go to them. Drop the phone and delay your next text, email, or post, and engage with them.

On your next daily delay or weekly withdrawal, share with your spouse the task you dropped and the person you engaged. Discuss the conversation highlights and the feeling you had when you walked away.

Let's PRAY about It

Prioritizing prayer will bring you closer together and pave the way for God to work in your life and relationship. Use the following prayer as a jumping-off point.

Lord, give us your heart for people. Slow us down to see people and their value. We want to live each day with margin for holy interruptions. We ask that the Holy Spirit call us by name so we'll notice when we sacrifice time with the most important people in our lives for tasks. We refuse to let tasks trump people. We thank you for the people and relationships you have surrounded us with. We pray this in the mighty name of Jesus. Amen.

Week 20

SLOW DOWN

Six days you shall labor and do all your work, but the
seventh day is a sabbath to the LORD your God.
Exodus 20:9–10

When our daughter was six, I was in a rush to get home and get cleaned up before the kids' soccer practice. I made a beeline for the restroom and noticed we were out of toilet paper. So I ran to another bathroom to find the Charmin. I grabbed a fresh roll and left it on the bathtub.

Later that night as the kids bathed, that roll fell into the tub. My daughter, in an effort to dispose of it, flushed the entire roll of double-quilted, double-roll toilet paper.

She came into my office and said, "Daddy, the toilet is overflowing." I rushed into the bathroom, and sure enough, she was right.

I did what you would probably do. I said, "That's okay, honey." Yeah, right! After I overreacted, we got the plunger and cleaned things up.

Corynn felt awful. I will never forget her words. "I'm stupid, ain't I?"

"Corynn," I said, "you are not stupid. Daddy overreacted. No way are you stupid."

The next morning, I woke up, and it gripped me again. So I went to Corynn's room and said, "Corynn, can I talk to you about last night and about the toilet?"

The first words out of her mouth were, "Daddy, I said I was sorry."

"Corynn, I want you to hear this again. I apologized last night, and I am going to apologize again. Daddy overreacted. This house means nothing to me. Toilets are not important. But you are so important to Daddy."

I sighed. "Daddy needs to not react so badly to this type of stuff. And just to help me practice, do you want to go flush another roll of toilet paper down the toilet? Let's do it, just me and you. We'll cut it into pieces and maybe do more than one flush to try to get the whole thing down. What do you say?"

We did not do it, but the point was clear: all this chaos, frustration, offense, and apology were the direct result of my hurry. We run too fast. It has been said that hurry kills the soul. It also kills the family and hinders our relationship with God.

The command for Sabbath rest is the longest of the Ten Commandments:

> Six days you shall labor and do all your work, but the seventh day is a sabbath to the LORD your God. On it you shall not do any work, neither you, nor your son or daughter, nor your male or female servant, nor your animals, nor any foreigner residing in your towns. For in six days the LORD made the heavens and the earth, the sea, and all that is in them, but he rested on the seventh day. Therefore the LORD blessed the Sabbath day and made it holy. (Ex. 20:9–11)

Jesus fulfilled all the Law, which means we are no longer bound by the commandment to cease all labor from sunset Friday night to sunset Saturday night. However, the principle of the Sabbath is still necessary. It is rest for our bodies, minds, and souls.

Take a break vocationally. "Remember the Sabbath day by keeping it holy" (Ex. 20:8). *Holy* means set apart. The Sabbath should look nothing like the other six days of the week. It has a different pace and rhythm. Close your laptop and let the calls go to voice mail. Sabbath rest encourages productivity during the workweek, since you are more rested for it.

Take a break physically, mentally, and emotionally. Highly productive people feel guilty even thinking about a nap. Lie down without setting an alarm. Read a novel instead of a textbook. Take a walk around the neighborhood.

Sabbath is not only for rest but also for worship. View it as unhurried time for worship, prayer, Bible reading, memorization, meditation, and devotions. Spend this time with the Lord, your spouse, and your family.

> ## Sabbath rest is our way of acknowledging that we are not God.

There is one place where I completely disconnect from work and rest my mind, heart, and body. When I am on the water, whether boating on the lake or wading in a river, I forget about the tasks and responsibilities of the week. Find your place and retreat there.

Sabbath rest is our way of acknowledging that we are not God. The earth still spins on its axis when we take twenty-four hours off. When I do not take the rest, I am touchy and on edge the other six days of the week. My kids and wife feel it. This is a time I must set apart to rest myself and bless my family.

Let's TALK about It

Discuss the following conversation starters and questions together, today or throughout the week.

- Describe the pace of your home (check all that apply):
  __ Frantic
  __ Balanced
  __ Healthy
  __ Unhealthy
  __ Relaxed
  __ Procrastinating
  __ Frustrated
  __ Exhausted
  __ Empty
  __ Full
- Does rest come easily for you?
- What keeps you from taking a full day of rest?
- Which day of the week works best for your Sabbath together?

Let's DO Something about It

Plan a twenty-four-hour period to take a Sabbath in the next seven days. If your week is already planned, try this in the next few weeks.

- Pick a day and time to start and end.
- Get your errands and household chores done before the Sabbath.

- Plan your menu for that day and purchase groceries ahead of time.
- Ask each member of your family what refreshing and restorative activities they'd like to do that day.
- Create a worship playlist to listen to throughout the day.
- Go back through this devotional and pick a week that resonated with you, and share it with the family.
- At the end of your Sabbath, revisit the questions from above and assess the day.

Let's PRAY about It

Prioritizing prayer will bring you closer together and pave the way for God to work in your life and relationship. Use the following prayer as a jumping-off point.

Lord, you are our refuge. In you we find rest. Slow the pace of our home, hearts, minds, and bodies. When we get anxious, reassure us that rest is for our good. Make this a discipline in our marriage and home. Use this rest to strengthen our marriage. We ask these things in Jesus' name. Amen.

IF TOMORROW NEVER COMES

A good name is better than fine perfume,
and the day of death better than the day of birth.
It is better to go to a house of mourning
than to go to a house of feasting,
for death is the destiny of everyone;
the living should take this to heart.

Ecclesiastes 7:1–2

Funerals are recalibrating events. You leave them changed, or at least you should. When you go to a funeral, you take to heart the death of someone you know and love.

Solomon observes that the "house of mourning" is where we come face to face with our own mortality. He writes that "the day of death [is] better than the day of birth" (Eccl. 7:1). Why? Perhaps because in the house of mourning, we ask important questions about God and life. When faced with the reality of our own death, we ask, "How am I living?" "How am I loving?" "Do I know the Lord?" "Am I walking closely with Jesus?"

I officiate a lot of funerals. After the funeral of, say, a young mom who lost the fight to cancer, I go home and hold Amy a little tighter.

I once preached the graveside sermon of a baby who had died from sudden infant death syndrome (SIDS). It completely changed the way I viewed my kids' messes and the chaos of our home.

Most funerals include a eulogy or time for family members to share about their loved one. They tell stories and memories, all while speaking words of high value. There are laughs and tears. It gets me every time. I believe one of life's greatest tragedies is to wait for a funeral to share words of high value over the ones we love.

From the front row of a funeral, I ask myself, "Did their loved one hear these words over the years?" Do not wait for a funeral to speak value over the people you love. Speak honor over them while they are with you.

I promised you no more Toby Keith songs, but I never said no more country music. Garth Brooks's classic lyric "If tomorrow never comes, will she know how much I love her?" is in my top-five favorite lyrics of all time.* Amy hears it often, both from Garth and from me. If I'm not singing it, it is on repeat in my truck.

I promise you this: when the Lord calls me home, I will have left no words unspoken. Those around me know how much I love and value them. I tell them often.

Do not wait for a funeral to speak value over the people you love.

Make a practice out of speaking words of high value over those you love. Do it so often that they say, "I know. I know. You tell me all

---

* Garth Brooks, vocalist, "If Tomorrow Never Comes," by Garth Brooks and Kent Blazy, released August 21, 1989, on *Garth Brooks*, Capitol Nashville 444.

the time." If your children roll their eyes in jest when you say it, you are right on track. Do not take your foot off the gas. Pedal to the metal on speaking words of honor.

Live out the lyrics of Tim McGraw's "Live Like You Were Dying." Live each day as though it is your last and as if you have people in your life who need to know how much you love and care for them. Say it now. Do not wait.

Let's TALK about It

Discuss the following questions together, today or throughout the week.

- Why do you think people wait for a funeral to speak words of high value over those they love?
- What are some of the most honoring words you have heard at a funeral?
- Did the last funeral you were a part of change you? In what ways?
- Who do we know who speaks honor over us often?
- What do you want said about you at your funeral?

Let's DO Something about It

My family accuses me of talking about death too much. Maybe because I have the order of service planned for my funeral, and I even have the start to my slide show. Morbid? Maybe, but I don't fear death. The teacher in me wants people at my funeral to take their own lives seriously as they take my death to heart.

Start a list of what you would like to have said about you at your funeral. The secret is you want to live up to your eulogy starting now. Share this with each other. It is an opportunity for you to bless your spouse and for your spouse to bless you, in the here and now.

Let's PRAY about It

Prioritizing prayer will bring you closer together and pave the way for God to work in your life and relationship. Use the following prayer as a jumping-off point.

Father, teach us to value our time together and take our own lives to heart. We take to heart our own destiny of death. We want to live each day as though you are coming back today or as though this could be our last breath. We will not hold back from you and those we love. They will know of our love for them. May we have our heads on a swivel, looking for ways to speak our love and words of high value over them each day. We pray this in the good name of Jesus. Amen.

PERSONALLY AUTOGRAPHED BY GOD

So God created mankind in his own image,
in the image of God he created them;
male and female he created them.

Genesis 1:27

You are created by God and for God. He created you for his purposes. So it is with everyone else, as well. To honor the image of God in men and women, we must see every human being as personally autographed by God and highly valuable.

We tend to value people based on their age, status, income, race, political party, marital status, immigration status, abilities, disabilities, intelligence, and doctrinal alignment with us. However, honoring the image of God in men and women means we value those who *don't* look like us, talk like us, believe like us, or vote like us ... because they too are image bearers of almighty God.

Your value comes from God, not from me or anyone else. Nothing I say or do can add to or take away from your value. Since God set your value, I can only recognize and appreciate it. That is honor. When I do not treat you as an image bearer of God, I dishonor you. But just because someone dishonors you doesn't mean your value changes.

Honor was my late mentor's favorite topic to teach. Dr. Gary Smalley defined honor as the decision to place high value, worth, and importance on another person. He told me often, "Always make honor one of your keynote talks. You can never go wrong reminding people of their value."

Truett Cathy, the founder of Chick-fil-A, claimed Proverbs 22:1 as his life verse: "A good name is more desirable than great riches; to be esteemed is better than silver or gold."

You know that special feeling you get when someone at Chick-fil-A says, "My pleasure," and means it? That is honor. It almost makes eating fried chicken seem like it is good for you. Esteeming people as highly valuable is priceless. It is truly "better than silver or gold."

When was the last time you reminded your spouse how valuable they are? Do your eyes light up when they walk into the room?

Do *you* get regular reminders of your value? Has anyone ever told you that you are not valuable? Did you believe them?

One of the most practical tools Gary ever taught Amy and me was what he called "the honor list." We took the time years ago to write down all the reasons we consider our spouse highly valuable. We use anniversaries and birthdays to add to the list each year. The sentiments of a thousand Hallmark cards pale in comparison to one line spoken from a well-thought-out honor list.

Here are three keys for best use of an honor list:

Write it. It takes only a few lines to get started. Do not labor over lofty words. Speak plainly.

Gift it. Instead of buying a card with someone else's thoughts, share items from the list on your next anniversary or special occasion.

Speak it. If you want to take the honor list up a notch, speak it out loud in front of family and friends. I share honor lists at birthday parties of friends and family members, and someone reaches for a tissue every time.

The first time I saw Gary's honor list for his wife, I noticed that he had four full pages of bullet points. When I asked him about it, he said, "After Norma and I get into conflict, I like to go in my home office and read a few lines from the list. It reminds me of her value and resets my mood."

He then added with a sheepish grin, "After conflict, don't edit the list—only read it."

One of the best ways to teach your children to honor God, others, and you is to honor each other. Honor begins at home. Let it begin with your marriage.

Let's TALK about It

Discuss the following questions together, today or throughout the week.

- Thinking back over your childhood, who spoke words of high value over you? What is one thing they said?
- Do you remember a time when you felt insecure or worthless and someone spoke a word of honor over you? What did they say? How did those words change you?
- Name a few roadblocks that keep us from honoring others.

Let's DO Something about It

Let's get the honor list started with three to five bullet points about your spouse's value. Fill in the blanks with the first word that comes to mind. Take turns doing this individually, then read it out loud to your spouse.

My favorite part of your personality is _____

_____

_____.

You place my needs before yours when you _____

_____

_____.

I smile every time I think about your willingness to _____

_____

_____.

When I'm discouraged, you lift me right up when you _____

_____

_____.

You make me laugh when you _____

_____

_____.

Throughout the rest of this devotional, grow your honor lists. Return to this list for additions or start a fresh list in a journal or in the notes on your phone.

Let's PRAY about It

Prioritizing prayer will bring you closer together and pave the way for God to work in your life and relationship. Use the following prayer as a jumping-off point.

Father, my spouse is fearfully and wonderfully made in your image and is highly valuable. Give us eyes to see each other with the value you gave us when you created us. You do not make junk, and we never want to treat each other as such. Give us the words each day to remind one another of our value in you. We love you, and it is in Jesus' name that we pray. Amen.

MALE AND FEMALE

*"Haven't you read," he replied, "that at the beginning
the Creator 'made them male and female'?"*

Matthew 19:4

After he created male and female, "God blessed them and said to them, 'Be fruitful and increase in number; fill the earth and subdue it. Rule over the fish in the sea and the birds in the sky and over every living creature that moves on the ground'" (Gen. 1:28). It is impossible to increase in number and fill the earth apart from the complementary design of male and female. Celebrating the created differences between men and women honors the image of God and his plan to fill the earth.

No need to fight against each other or our differences. Our complementary design makes each other better. We are equal yet different. Our differences bond us and create oneness. Perhaps you have heard it said, "If your spouse were just like you, one of you would not be needed."

A quick study of a high school anatomy book shows that God created our bones, muscles, and skeletal structure in unique ways. For example, a man's bicep attaches to his frame differently than a woman's bicep attaches. This gives the man more torque. The first time I learned that I thought, "God, you made men to open jars."

Nothing brings me greater joy in the kitchen than to have Amy hand me a jar she cannot open. Nine times out of ten, I open it and flex my bicep. She gives me a little squeeze.

However, one jar out of ten gives me trouble. A quick run of the jar under hot water followed by a few light taps with the handle of a butter knife usually does the trick. But nothing takes the wind out of a man's sails like handing the unopened jar back to his wife after several failed attempts and watching her open it with ease. In that case, Amy gently says, "You got it started for me. Thank you!" I married a precious woman.

Our differences are on display all around our home. Amy and I bought our first home in 1998 while I was attending seminary in Dallas. It was one of those $90,000 cookie-cutter houses in a subdivision of two hundred homes. We got to choose some upgrades, but most of the features of the house were what everyone else in the subdivision got.

One night shortly after moving in, Amy and I were enjoying an evening at home watching one of our favorite television shows. Halfway through the program, Amy jumped up and announced, "I can't sit in this living room one more minute!"

"What's wrong?" I asked.

"Doesn't it bother you that the doorknobs in this room are polished brass and the ceiling fan is brushed nickel? What were the builders thinking?"

My eyes focused on the fan, then the door, then the fan, and then the door in rapid fire. I could not process her panic. I had no idea that for the first thirty minutes of the show we'd watched that night, Amy could not focus on the plot or the characters because of the mismatched doorknobs and ceiling fan.

I'll bet you can guess what our first errand was that Saturday. Correct: we were at Home Depot purchasing brushed-nickel doorknobs. Afterward, Amy was at peace.

Well, she *was* ... until she walked into the bedroom that night. You see, one of the new doorknobs was on a door between our bedroom and the living room. The ceiling fan in our master bedroom was polished brass.

On Sunday, we went back to Home Depot and purchased a brushed-nickel ceiling fan.

The home is an extension of the wife, whereas a man can more easily detach from his surroundings. I can sit comfortably and relax in a cluttered room. Amy must pick up some dog toys and straighten out the pillows before relaxing. We work it out.

Some Christian leaders believe we have overblown the differences between men and women. While that may be true to some extent, do not let the pendulum swing too far to the other side. We must not dismiss the differences altogether because acknowledging our complementary design is a way to honor the God who made us.

Let's TALK about It

Discuss the following questions together, today or throughout the week.

- What are some of the differences between male and female on display in our marriage and home?
- Can you think of a recent story where the differences between male and female caused conflict in our relationship? What did we do to reconcile this conflict?
- Name a few ways culture drifts from the truth that men and women are created equal but different.

Let's DO Something about It

Recognizing and celebrating the created differences between men and women provides great content for the honor list you have started keeping on your spouse. Fill in the blanks below to add to your list:

You show me love and care when you _____

_____

_____ .

When I'm hurting, I appreciate it when you _____

_____

_____ .

Around the house, you are most helpful when you _____

_____ .

You make driving in the car fun every time you _____

_____ .

I love watching _____ with
you because you almost always _____

_____ .

Let's PRAY about It

Prioritizing prayer will bring you closer together and pave the way for God to work in your life and relationship. Use the following prayer as a jumping-off point.

Lord, we are grateful for our created differences. As culture drifts from your truth and seeks to blur the line between male and female, keep our marriage grounded in your Word and the truth. As we see the beauty in the way you wired each one of us, give us the words to call it out and honor one another in it. May we honor you by honoring each other. We love you, and it is in Jesus' holy name we pray. Amen.

CHECK THE GAUGES

*Stop drinking only water, and use a little wine because
of your stomach and your frequent illnesses.*

1 Timothy 5:23

In this verse, Paul gives us a beautiful example of pastoral care. He knew the connection between physical wellness and ministry effectiveness. Our wellness affects our performance. Timothy's calling and assignment were too important for Timothy to be out of commission, and Paul wanted him healthy for the sake of his own soul and the Lord's work.

I don't know where I would be today had I not received care and accountability from a Paul in my life. As a young pastor, like Timothy, I was blessed with a seasoned minister who kept me in check.

The spring of 2007 ushered in one of the most stressful seasons of our marriage and ministry. After having saved for ten years, Amy and I invested our nest egg into building our dream home. We decided to complete the build before listing the house we occupied. I told Amy, "The housing market is so strong, it will sell in no time." About three weeks after we moved into our new home and listed the old one, the bad news about the housing market surfaced. Within a month, we heard the term *recession*. We were left with two mortgage payments on houses with decreasing value. During this time, we also had a significant betrayal in the ministry.

Those were dark months. I woke up each morning at 1:00 or 2:00 a.m. and sat at the end of our bed. I prayed a lot but, honestly, I spent most of the time stressing and worrying. I would commit our home, family, and ministry to the Lord, but seconds later my mind raced with all the ways we could lose everything. I lost sleep, gained weight, and stopped caring for my overall wellness.

By God's grace, he surrounded me with godly men and women who cared, called me out, and helped me get healthy. Dr. Gary Smalley was an elder at our church at this time, and he walked alongside me through these trials. We traveled together often, and Gary used meals, flights, and drives to ask me questions that kept my heart, mind, and body in check. I can still see him counting on his fingers as he asked me about each area of my life.

Gary went home to be with the Lord more than six years ago, but I still use these questions as gauges in my marriage, family, and ministry.

- **Physical Gauge:** Am I getting close to eight hours of sleep a night, eating well, and resting when tired? Do I take one full day off every week? Am I exercising? Am I honoring God with my body (1 Cor. 6:19–20)?
- **Emotional Gauge:** Is my heart open or closed? Is my anger, anxiety, or irritability caused by hurt, fear, or frustration? Anger is a secondary emotion, so identify your primary feeling (usually fear). When was the last time you laughed?
- **Relational Gauge:** A closed heart leads to isolation. Do I have trusted friends who need more access to my life? Is there anyone in my life I need

to forgive in my heart or from whom I need to seek forgiveness?

- **Mental Gauge:** Am I able to check out from work and let my mind be at ease? What am I studying to keep my mind sharp? What habits are dumbing me down?
- **Vocational Gauge:** Do I find satisfaction in my work? Am I doing my work for the Lord or for me? Am I working too many hours? Has work become my source of life?
- **Financial Gauge:** Do I give generously, spend wisely, avoid debt, and save? Do I spend less than I make? What areas of discretionary spending can I cut back on?
- **Marital Gauge:** Are we keeping our daily delay, weekly withdrawal, and annual abandon? Am I intoxicated with the love of my wife (see Prov. 5:19)?
- **Spiritual Gauge:** Do I regularly confess sin, spend time in Scripture, and pray? Am I plugged into a biblical community and serving my local church? Am I growing in my faith?

Greater joy requires a constant checkup on your physical, emotional, relational, mental, vocational, financial, marital, and spiritual gauges. When one of these is out of balance, it throws off all the others.

If you are not getting the sleep your body needs, for example, it will drain you emotionally, and you will be snappy with your family and friends. If your emotional health is suffering, your toxicity will isolate you from your most important relationships. A crisis in your vocation can lead to financial stress. A financial emergency can lead to impulsive rather than principled decisions, and that results in the degradation of your soul, marriage, and walk with Christ.

Let's TALK about It

Discuss the following questions together, today or throughout the week.

- Can you think of a time in our marriage when we neglected one or more of these gauges?
- How about a time when we seemed most healthy across the board?
- Which gauge(s) needs our attention as a couple?

Let's DO Something about It

In the space on the next page or on a separate sheet of paper, draw a dashboard with all eight of these gauges. Model each one on the fuel gauge in your car, with E on the left and F on the right (or however your car's fuel gauge looks).

Individually, draw a needle on each gauge where you believe you and your marriage are currently. *Empty* is running on fumes and needs your immediate attention. *Full* is doing great.

Keep the dashboard out for the next week and make a plan to move each needle toward *Full*.

Let's PRAY about It

Prioritizing prayer will bring you closer together and pave the way for God to work in your life and relationship. Use the following prayer as a jumping-off point.

Father, all these gauges start with our relationship with you. When we are full of your love, we have all we need to move the other gauges up. Call out in us the areas of our marriage that are headed in the wrong direction. We want nothing in our marriage to move the needle toward empty with you. Fill us. We know and rely on the love you have for us. We praise you for your love. In Jesus' name. Amen.

Week 25

CAMPING AND SCHEDULED DISASTERS

Consider it pure joy, my brothers and sisters, whenever you face trials of many kinds, because you know that the testing of your faith produces perseverance. Let perseverance finish its work so that you may be mature and complete, not lacking anything.

James 1:2–4

Dr. Gary Smalley considered camping to be the secret to a close-knit family. He had an entire talk in his marriage seminar detailing the camping disasters he'd experienced with his family. For years, he encouraged Amy and me to buy a camper and to schedule camping trips on weekends. Like a bass on a Rapala lure, we took the bait.

Something always goes wrong when camping. Seasoned campers testify that the best stories come out of the trips with storms, accidents, or conflict. We have friends with stories ranging from catching their tent on fire to hitting a moose head-on at seventy-five miles per hour and totaling their RV.

Amy and I bought a twenty-two-foot Outback camper when Corynn was nine months old, and we spent two weeks traveling across the great state of Arkansas. The opening night of our trip was actually spent in a hotel because I was too tired to check in at the KOA and set up. This was our first clue that camping was not for us.

On the third day of the trip, I backed the truck up too fast and hit the camper, knocking it back about three feet. Did I mention this was near a cliff? The camper was still about ten feet from the edge of the cliff, but Amy and Corynn were inside. Out of the side mirror, I saw Amy's head pop out of the door with eyes as big as saucers. Even when I wasn't almost knocking my loved ones over the ledge, connecting the ball to the hitch took a lot of practice.

Toward the end of the trip, I almost lost Amy, Corynn, and the camper a second time. I had decided to run to Walmart for supplies, and while I was gone, Amy accidentally brushed up against the stove. She opened the gas lines without lighting the burner. For an hour, the camper filled with gas and became one giant propane tank.

When I stepped back into the camper, the smell hit me in the face. I immediately grabbed my napping daughter and yelled for Amy to get out of the camper. We stood some distance from the camper, staying clear and blowing gently on Corynn's face. Everyone survived.

When Gary asked about the trip, I told him, "You need to change the title of your talk to 'Camping: Scheduled Disasters and Near-Death Experiences.'"

Despite this story, disasters are not the secret to quality time. Our responses, and how we work together as a team through the disasters—that is the secret. Life throws plenty of challenges our way. How we respond to these either moves us closer together or drives us apart.

Gary ended his talks on trials with a cheerleader's pom-pom in hand. He'd mention trials one at a time, and after each one, he'd raise the pom-pom and cheer, "Yay!" This was his precious way of rejoicing and celebrating the growth that comes from trials.

Amy and I sold our camper after that trip to Arkansas. We only day camp now. We rent a spot at State Park Marina, lounge around the fire, cook, walk, and play cards. She insists on being home by 10:00 p.m. so she can shower and sleep in our bed. I oblige.

Let's TALK about It

Discussion Questions for Outdoorsy Couples:

- What leisure activity or vacation causes you the most stress?
- List some of the essentials required for you to best enjoy camping or your favorite outdoor activity. (For example: not hiking in more than a mile, camping near a water source, using a pop-up versus tent camping, etc.)
- What is your favorite outdoor activity we do together?
- How often should we do that activity?

Discussion Questions for Indoorsy Couples:

- Do we have any outdoorsy friends who inspire us enough to consider joining them on one of their outdoor adventures?
- What part(s) of camping do you dislike the most?
- If you had to choose one outdoor activity to do for a few hours, what activity could you get excited about?
- Who among our outdoorsy friends should we invite to do this activity with us?

Let's DO Something about It

Plan a camping date. No overnight needed. Grab some lawn chairs, coolers, firewood, snacks, and drinks. For the full effect, consider renting a twenty-five-dollar campsite at a local campground. You might not experience disaster, but there will be hassles. Take the time on this date to discuss the Let's TALK about It questions.

Let's PRAY about It

Prioritizing prayer will bring you closer together and pave the way for God to work in your life and relationship. Use the following prayer as a jumping-off point.

Father, our joy is in you, not in the trial. For that reason, we look for you in every trial and hassle that comes our way. You are with us no matter what. Stretch our faith in you with each challenge and obstacle we face. Thank you for the opportunity to learn and grow from these trials. In the name of Jesus. Amen.

LUVE TALK

My dove in the clefts of the rock,
in the hiding places on the mountainside,
show me your face,
let me hear your voice;
for your voice is sweet,
and your face is lovely.

Song of Songs 2:14

Like many couples, Amy and I enjoy conversations from three rooms away. From the closet in our bedroom, she yells to me in the kitchen. I can tell there is a question in her tone, but her words sound like Charlie Brown's teacher: "Wah waah wah wah wah waah?"

Instead of coming together in the same room to talk, we repeat ourselves, louder. The cycle is usually three attempts before we give up and forget the conversation ever happened.

Solomon solves this for us when he refers to the Shulammite woman as a gentle, tender dove. She is hidden, and he wants her to come out. So he makes the request: "Show me your face, let me hear your voice."

A tip for husbands: Let your request be gentle and tender. Do not demand that she open up and talk to you. A soft voice and a simple request will keep the conversation flowing.

More importantly, when she does open up and share, be a safe listener. Let your response and tone echo Solomon's: "For your voice is sweet, and your face is lovely." Safety is the secret to intimacy. If you want to stay emotionally connected to your spouse, be a safe listener. Be gentle. Never demand, control, or manipulate the conversation.

Years ago, Amy and I learned about something our dear friend Dr. Shawn Stoever calls the LUVE talk. LUVE—listen, understand, validate, and empathize—changed everything about how we communicate. Let's take a look at each one.

- **Listen.** You listen best with your eyes wide open and your mouth shut. Remove all distractions and devices. Lean in, turn your head, and give your ear. Listening says, "You matter to me. You are important and worthy of my time." Listening does not mean "I agree with you." A healthy person is not threatened by the differing opinions and feelings of their spouse.

- **Understand.** There are two ways to show you "get it." One is to repeat back to your spouse word for word what they just said. Your spouse will let you know when your tone and nonverbal expressions— as well as the words—match what they said. Do not quit early. Sometimes, it takes a few times back and forth for understanding to come. Another way is to ask questions for clarification. That helps draw out the understanding.

- **Validate.** Restaurants and stores validate your parking ticket with a stamp. It means "You were here." Validation in marriage is the stamp that says, "I was fully present for this conversation." Go for the stamp after your spouse shares by saying something like, "I hear what you're saying, and that must have been hard to hear."

- **Empathize.** Amy and I missed this in our conversation for years. Empathy says, "You are hurting, and that matters to me." This part of the LUVE talk does not solve a problem or fix something that is broken. None of the parts do, actually. You are simply entering into the opinions and feelings of your spouse.

Reread Song of Songs 2:14 above. I nicknamed Amy "My Dove" from this passage of Scripture. Instead of frustrating ourselves with long-distance conversations, I simply call for her. *Coo-coo-coo.* She knows that is me inviting her out into safety. I can meet her on the way to me or go to where she is. The dove call really says, "Let's get in the same room."

If you practice this level of emotional safety in your conversations, the door will always be open for you to share. Safety keeps our hearts open to one another.

Let's TALK about It

Discuss the following questions together, today or throughout the week.

- Is it hard to get my undivided attention?
- What is our biggest distraction as a couple when listening to each other?
- When we are locked in on each other, what about my body language and tone tells you I have understood what you are saying?

- What topic or issue in our marriage causes the most complications when it comes to communication?
- How can I be better available and validating for those conversations?

Let's DO Something about It

Set up two chairs face to face in the most wide-open space in your house.

Lean forward in your chairs and make eye contact without saying a word for thirty seconds straight.

How awkward was that?

Take turns on this next part.

Share with your spouse what frustrates you the most about other drivers on the road.

Let your spouse repeat back to you word for word what you just said. It's always good to start with "So what I hear you saying is …"

Did your tone, posture, and body language match what you said?

Repeat with a new topic. Keep it light for the first few and work your way up to topics that cause tension. Offer much grace in the process.

Let's PRAY about It

Prioritizing prayer will bring you closer together and pave the way for God to work in your life and relationship. Use the following prayer as a jumping-off point.

Lord, you listen to us every time we cry out to you. Your heart is to care for ours. Give us the same desire for one another. We want a heart-to-heart marriage, not a head-to-head one. Intimacy is being fully known and fully accepted. You know us and love us. We are safe with you. We want to know each other deeply and find safety when we share the intimate details of our lives. In Jesus' name. Amen.

LISTEN TO UNDERSTAND, NOT REPLY

Fools find no pleasure in understanding
but delight in airing their own opinions.

Proverbs 18:2

We get our news today from algorithms on social media and cable news networks that reinforce our biases. That means we primarily listen to and watch news that corresponds with our values. Our listening skills suffer as a result. Our grandparents watched the news to find out what was going on in the world, but now we tune in to find out what we should be mad about for the rest of the day.

Proverbs 18:2 says, "Fools find no pleasure in understanding but delight in airing their own opinions." It is okay to have your own opinions, but not at the expense of understanding others. For example, social media allows us to express our views without sticking around for the conversation to follow. We spew and then scroll to the next post. Proverbs 18:13 teaches, "To answer before listening—that is folly and shame." A person of understanding listens before expressing opinions, insight, or experience.

Have you seen the movie *Patch Adams*? In an early scene, Patch rushes into his therapist's office and announces that he would like to check out from the hospital because he has a goal: "I want to help people. I want to listen. I want to really listen to people." His therapist says, "That's what I do." Patch confronts him with the truth that he stinks at his job and says, "You don't even look at people when they talk to you." Ouch!

Understanding comes from better listening. To be a better listener, I need to be aware of some bad listening habits. Here are seven bad listening habits that threaten the safety of our conversations. Allow the following "bad listeners" to help you identify ways to improve your listening skills.

The **Nodder** is the listener who took a management course at work that taught how to seem emotionally responsive when someone is talking. As your spouse shares, it's good to give cues to let them know you are listening. But the Nodder takes it too far and gives a nod to each statement made. Excessive nodding can be a mark of insincere listening.

The **Eye-roller** shows contempt. In my opinion, out of the seven bad listeners on this list, this is the most disrespectful. Eye-rolling shoots right past your spouse's stories, ideas, or opinions and goes straight to their character. It attacks the core of their personhood. The eye-roll screams, "You don't matter!" or "You still don't get it."

The **Bored** listener does not show contempt but has a difficult time connecting with body language and facial expressions. The vibe is "I'd rather be somewhere else doing something else."

The **Distracted** listener comes in two forms. One, this person is distracted by their environment (people, devices, setting, etc.). Two, this person is distracted in their mind (thoughts, lists, errands, etc.). In either case, the lack of focus keeps this listener from dialing in to another's words and feelings.

The **Eye-wanderer** is on the lookout for something better to do or someone else to engage in conversation. This person looks over your shoulder to see who is coming. When an Eye-wanderer's eyes glaze over but then light up when someone else walks by, it is difficult not to take it personally.

The **Watch-glancer** checks the time during the conversation. As the little girl on *Full House* would say, "How rude!" A quick glance at the time says to your spouse, "I need you to wrap this up," or "You've taken enough of my time."

The **Bottom-liner** needs you to cut to the chase. This is a time-oriented listener who needs enough but not too much information to get the gist. Even if you are an excellent communicator and quickly get to the point, the Bottom-liner will cut you off when he or she feels you should be finished. Beyond the essentials, he or she only hears, "Blah, blah, blah."

May Amy never say of me, "You stink at listening. You do not even look at me when I talk to you." Instead, I want everything about my listening to say, "What you think and feel matters. You matter to me."

Let's TALK about It

Discuss the following questions together, today or throughout the week.

- Which of the seven bad-listener styles do you freely confess you struggle with most in marriage?
- Which listening type bothers you the most?
- Ask your spouse, "On a scale of one to ten, how am I doing as a listener?"
- What are some bad listening habits you need to cut out?

Let's DO Something about It

Compliment your spouse on the strengths of their listening. Check and share with your spouse all that apply.

___ ___ You keep great eye contact when I'm talking to you.

___ ___ You remove distractions when we need to talk.

___ ___ You are slow to respond and rarely interrupt.

___ ___ I love that you do not always have to be right.

___ ___ Thank you for turning toward me when I talk.

___ ___ You always keep the kids from interrupting me.

___ ___ You let me go first.

___ ___ I can tell when you are working to restrain your words, and I appreciate that.

___ ___ Even when you want to share your opinion, you are quick to let it go.

Let's PRAY about It

Prioritizing prayer will bring you closer together and pave the way for God to work in your life and relationship. Use the following prayer as a jumping-off point.

Father, may the Holy Spirit convict us when we are talking too much and not letting each other get a word in edgewise. Incline our ears to one another. Remove the strong desire to always be right. We want intimacy and connection more than winning and one-upping. We thank you for our marriage and for the opportunity to know each other deeply. In Jesus' name. Amen.

THE SIX LEVELS OF COMMUNICATION

The purpose in a man's heart is like deep water,
but a man of understanding will draw it out.

Proverbs 20:5 ESV

Marriage experts agree that there are many levels of communication. The deeper your communication, the greater your intimacy. There are six levels of communication, and the goal is to live at level six. This is the deepest level, where you find the strongest, most intimate connection within marriage.

Level 1 is small talk. This is the shallowest level of communication. It's the clichés we exchange with strangers in stores and servers in restaurants. We remain on this level with the family members and friends we want to keep at arm's length. There is zero risk of escalated argument at this level.

Level 2 is facts. At this level, we begin sharing basic personal information about our day, family, and work. Examples include, "I need to get the kids to school by eight tomorrow morning." "After work, I need to run a few errands." "I'll meet you tonight for dinner around seven." This too is a level with zero risk of escalated arguments. Healthy spouses share at this level with no toxicity.

Level 3 is opinions. Escalated arguments start and camp here. Opinions come out, such as "I think $200 is too much for groceries." "You're driving too fast." "You shouldn't have said that." Opinions start with facts and then place a value judgment on them. A fact is "I spent $200 on groceries." An opinion is "That is too much to spend on groceries."

Intimacy does not grow on levels 1 through 3. You must go deeper if you want intimacy. Draw a line right here in this book under level 3, and commit to being a below-the-line couple. Sure, levels 1 through 3 are necessary to catch up on the day, but do not live there. Commit to go deeper on a daily basis.

Level 4 is feelings. This level is not necessarily gushy. It is not about wearing your heart on your sleeve or crying. Feeling words include *loved, unloved, valued, devalued, cheated, accepted, unwanted, judged, connected,* and *disconnected.* When your spouse shares feeling words, do the hard work of understanding and validating those feelings.

Level 5 is desires and needs. Here, you share your desired outcome of the conversation. "I wish we could …" or "Wouldn't it be cool if we …" are two good ways to begin sharing your desires. This works only after you do the work of understanding at level 4, though. If you skip the feelings level and go straight to needs, you will tend to control or manipulate the conversation.

Level 6 is beliefs. This is where you discover where the feelings, opinions, and desires come from. Beliefs are messages written on the heart. A belief may be something that someone said or did to us over a long period of time. Examples include statements such as "Why can't you be more like your brother." "I've told you a thousand times …" "You were a mistake." Once we accept those messages as truth, they guide our lives. We act, react, and speak straight from these messages.

Certainly, some beliefs come from hearing recurring messages, as I said, but some do not. I may believe something about myself based on a onetime trauma. I may believe something because someone trustworthy told me once. I may believe something from repeated experience, such as trusting that a chair I've never seen before will hold me up based on other sitting experiences.

Every message written on the heart has a story attached to it. Something a parent or teacher said over and over again about you and you eventually believed it. A message or song you heard growing up that shaped your life. A bully who called you a name and it stuck with you.

Praise God, this is the level where he does work within us. Even if a parent, sibling, spouse, ex-spouse, coach, or pastor lied to us for years about our personhood or value, God speaks truth. He doesn't change us on the opinions or facts level—he moves in our hearts!

When Amy and I share at level 6, it gives us a glimpse into each other's journey. Above the line is about winning and getting your point of view across to your spouse. Below the line says, "I want to get to know you." It is not about winning an argument. It is about diving deep into the sacred places of your spouse's heart.

Let's TALK about It

Discuss the following questions together, today or throughout the week.

- How would you describe your communication style?
- Are we an above-the-line or a below-the-line couple?
- What needs to change in order for us to get or stay below the line?
- Are there any couples we know who practice below-the-line communication well? What can we learn from them?

Let's DO Something about It

On a blank sheet of paper, write the six levels of communication on the left-hand side, from top to bottom. Talk through the details of a major decision you need to make for your marriage, home, or work. Jot down your thoughts next to each level as you identify each one. Work to stay below the line in the conversation.

Use "I feel ..." sentences more than "I think ..." sentences. When your conversation reminds you of a story from childhood, share it. This is an activity to carry with you throughout the week. If the decision is not pressing, it does not need to be made tonight. Give it time.

Let's PRAY about It

Prioritizing prayer will bring you closer together and pave the way for God to work in your life and relationship. Use the following prayer as a jumping-off point.

Jesus, I confess with my mouth that you are Lord and believe in my heart that you have been raised from the dead. I want a deep relationship with you, one where I share what is deep in my heart. May I never hold back from you. You know my heart. "Search me, God, and know my heart; test me and know my anxious thoughts. See if there is any offensive way in me, and lead me in the way everlasting" (Ps. 139:23–24). In Jesus' name. Amen.

KIND WORDS

Kind words are like honey—
sweet to the soul and healthy for the body.

Proverbs 16:24 NLT

I was relentlessly picked on in junior high for having a larger-than-normal-size head and carrying a few extra pounds. The words of my classmates were cruel. They crushed me daily. We recover from bruises and broken bones caused by sticks and stones way faster than the wounds caused by cutting, unkind words.

My mom had a saying that she yelled up the stairs to me almost every morning on her way to work: "Don't let the turkeys get you down."

Oddly, I took great comfort in those words.

She also loved to say, "Kill 'em with kindness," which has origins in a fifteenth-century proverb about a mother ape crushing her newborn with a hug. Okay, that is a bit weird, but I love the sentiment.

I am no longer in junior high, but the world still hurls insults, jabs, and accusations at me, as I'm sure it does at you, as well. Amy is now my defender. She is a kind wife who knows the words I need to hear at the time I need to hear them.

Kindness does not require mushy or tear-filled words. It does not mean you speak like a Hallmark Channel movie script. Kind words send comfort straight to the heart of your spouse.

Kindness kills our insecurities. In the Song of Songs, we read that the Shulammite woman was insecure about her body and her family.

> Dark am I, yet lovely,
>   daughters of Jerusalem,
> dark like the tents of Kedar,
>   like the tent curtains of Solomon.
> Do not stare at me because I am dark,
>   because I am darkened by the sun.
> My mother's sons were angry with me
>   and made me take care of the vineyards;
>   my own vineyard I had to neglect. (1:5–6)

In that day, paleness was beauty. Her tanned skin meant she labored in the fields. She uses the vineyard both literally and figuratively. Her dysfunctional family forced her to work in the vineyard, which caused her to neglect her body.

Solomon responds with a word picture from his day to speak directly to her insecurities and praise his love's beauty:

> I liken you, my darling, to a mare
>   among Pharaoh's chariot horses.
> Your cheeks are beautiful with earrings,
>   your neck with strings of jewels.
> We will make you earrings of gold,
>   studded with silver. (vv. 9–11)

Pro tip: Comparing your spouse to a tent, horse, or young goat is not a good idea … unless you lived in Solomon's day. When Solomon likened his lover to the mare among Pharaoh's chariots, he was using an emotional word picture to communicate the fact that she was the most important woman in his life. When Pharaoh showed up to battle in his chariot, a white mare pulled his chariot, while dark horses pulled all the other chariots. In making this comparison, Solomon said that this woman stands out beautifully to him above all other women.

Kind words are gentle and healing. They must be more than trite, blanket statements. They look for wounds, hurts, and insecurities to speak truth over them. Greater joy together is found when we speak healing words to each other to cover the lies of the world.

Let's TALK about It

Discuss the following questions together, today or throughout the week.

- What are the kindest words a teacher, coach, pastor, relative, or parent ever shared with you as a child?
- Practically speaking, how can we praise the beauty of the women in this family?
- Why is it important for a woman to know she is beautiful?
- What are some of the lies Satan speaks over women about their bodies and beauty?
- Is our marriage a safe place filled with kind words?

Let's DO Something about It

Each of you has experienced an insecurity that comes from a lie or destructive word someone in the past spoke over you. Tell a story about how those unkind words affected you.

Now, speak to each other sincere, kind words that oppose those lies. Use a word picture. Leave sticky notes around the house throughout the week with those kind words written on them. Text kindness to each other. Include those words in your prayer for each other before you drift off to sleep tonight. Speak those words to each other in front of your children or grandchildren. Let the world know the truth about your spouse.

Let's PRAY about It

Prioritizing prayer will bring you closer together and pave the way for God to work in your life and relationship. Use the following prayer as a jumping-off point.

Father, your loving-kindness is better than life. You expressed the ultimate kindness to us through Christ Jesus. He brings us life. May our words bring life and healing to this marriage. We rebuke the lies spoken over us in the past. We will not speak lies over each other. This marriage and home will be a safe place where we both flourish individually and together. It is in Jesus' name that we pray. Amen.

RESOLVING UNMET EXPECTATIONS

An angry person stirs up conflict,
and a hot-tempered person commits many sins.
Proverbs 29:22

Stress is the socially acceptable term for *anger*. It is the gap between what you expect and what you receive. No one can brag about being angry, so we call it stress.

James asks, "What causes fights and quarrels among you? Don't they come from your desires that battle within you?" (James 4:1). He then answers, "You desire but do not have, so you kill. You covet but you cannot get what you want, so you quarrel and fight. You do not have because you do not ask God" (v. 2). When we don't get our way, we get angry and stir up strife. But there is a better way to navigate these waters.

Start by bringing your expectations to the surface. Make a list of the expectations you brought to marriage. Then answer three questions for each one:

- Do I need to change or adjust this expectation?
- Is my expectation fair and reasonable?

- If I express my expectation, will my spouse find it reasonable?

The key here is to *address one expectation at a time.* When all expectations are clumped together, one grade is assigned. This is problematic. There's a reason your report cards at school gave separate grades for math, reading, science, music, social studies, and physical education. You were graded on your work in each individual class. Some of us did well in reading and music but did poorly in math and science. Individual grades help us focus and place more energy where it needs to be directed, and they do so without overwhelming us.

Bottom line: your various expectations about marriage need individual categories on your report card. Address them one at a time.

I do not want you to be an underachiever or an overexpecter as a spouse. Work on what you can change, and release what you cannot. Guess what you can change. You! You can totally change yourself and your expectations. But you cannot change all your reality on your own.

Remember, you are responsible for the expectations you bring to marriage. You may need to confess to your spouse that you have been expecting too much. Letting your spouse off the hook will change the atmosphere of your home. Not only will you walk a little lighter, but your spouse will too.

The key to resolving these unmet expectations is to take personal responsibility for your own expectations.

Finally, align your expectations with reality. The goal is that you will be able to create new, realistic, and biblical expectations for the future. Your spouse and children need this. You need this.

The key to resolving these unmet expectations is to take personal responsibility for your own expectations. Stop trying to adjust the behavior of your spouse. The gap between what we expect and what we experience drains our energy. As you begin to understand God's expectation for you and your marriage, his Spirit will reveal and convict you of areas that require change. God gives you the power to change yourself. You need to trust and believe that God works in the lives of others to grow and change them in ways you cannot control.

Let's TALK about It

Discuss the following questions together, today or throughout the week.

- Share with your spouse some of the unfair, unreasonable expectations you brought into marriage.
- How did you release or adjust those expectations over time?
- Are there any unmet expectations in your relationship at the moment?
- Are there any reasonable, fair expectations in your spouse's mind that you could step up to the plate and start meeting?

Let's DO Something about It

Differentiating between healthy, realistic expectations and negotiable ones is vital for future expectations we may place on each other. In the space below, write some expectations in each category and discuss for the future. There will be some you release and others you may choose to meet.

Healthy Expectations	Negotiable Expectations
_____	_____
_____	_____
_____	_____
_____	_____
_____	_____
_____	_____
_____	_____
_____	_____

Let's PRAY about It

Prioritizing prayer will bring you closer together and pave the way for God to work in your life and relationship. Use the following prayer as a jumping-off point.

Father, when I begin to expect too much of my spouse, I want to release those expectations. When I can meet the expectations of my spouse, guard me from becoming selfish and stubborn and refusing to do so. We seek open lines of communication to share freely what we expect and what we release. There is great joy in letting our spouse off the hook. Deal with us personally so we do not blame each other for the desires that war within us. We thank you for the opportunity to honor one another through our expectations in marriage. We love you and ask these things in Jesus' name. Amen.

APOLOGIES THAT BRING LIFE

The tongue has the power of life and death,
and those who love it will eat its fruit.

Proverbs 18:21

A friend once told me, "There are three very difficult things to say in life: 'I'm sorry,' 'I was wrong,' and 'Worcestershire sauce.'"

Reconciling in marriage requires giving and receiving apologies. Crafting a heartfelt apology takes time and effort. But strained relationships need words that bring healing, not strife and more destruction.

Why do our mouths get us into so much trouble? James tells us that the tongue determines the direction and quality of your life and relationships:

> When we put *bits* into the mouths of horses to make them obey us, we can turn the whole animal. Or take ships as an example. Although they are so large and are driven by strong winds, they are steered by a *very small rudder* wherever the pilot wants to go. Likewise, the tongue is a small part of the body, but it makes

great boasts. Consider what a great forest is set on
fire by a small spark. The tongue also is a *fire*, a world
of evil among the parts of the body. It corrupts the
whole body, sets the whole course of one's life on fire,
and is itself set on fire by hell. (James 3:3–6)

The tongue is a such a small part of the body, but it "has the power
of life and death" (Prov. 18:21). It restores, heals, builds up, soothes,
and reconciles. It can also tear down, destroy, ruin, and kill.

When our tongues bring words of death to the marriage, we need
life-giving apologies to reconcile. Here are a few practical considerations to help us do just that.

First, make sure it is helpful. When I flippantly say to my wife,
"I'm sorry," it usually means I just want the conflict to be over. That
is my flight response. In our early years of marriage, Amy pressed for
more. "You're sorry for what?" she'd ask.

Twenty-five years into marriage, I now automatically tag my "I'm
sorry" with the word or action that was wrong.

Also, if I say, "I'm sorry you feel that way," I invalidate her feelings, and the meaning is more like, "You shouldn't feel that way." You
should never apologize for the way someone feels. Apologize for your
words and actions.

When you say, "If I offended you, I'm sorry," you're telling the
other person, "You're too sensitive."

"I'm sorry that you took it that way," is interpreted as, "You read
more into that than I intended." You are really blaming your spouse for
bad understanding rather than taking responsibility for poor delivery.

Second, use fewer words. The Bible tells us that a wise man
restrains his words. A well-crafted apology is short and straight to
the point. You do not need to offer a dissertation on the situation.

State the offense and take ownership for your part of the conflict. The Bible reminds us, "Fire goes out for lack of fuel" (Prov. 26:20 TLB). A concise, well-crafted apology does not add fuel to the fire of the dispute.

Third, if possible, apologize in person. Text messages, emails, and phone calls are okay but often lack the full meaning that would be conveyed through your nonverbals if you were there in person. When I apologize, I want to know that it lands on Amy's heart. Texting an apology and watching those three dots is excruciating. When you apologize face to face, you get to watch the other person's reception of it in real time to make sure it has been effective.

Finally, ask for forgiveness. Sometimes, we can minimize the pain that another's words or actions caused us. We say things like, "It's no big deal," "I wasn't offended," or "Don't give it a second thought."

For some people, "I forgive you" ought to be on the list of difficult things to say. "I forgive you" can be just as difficult to say as "I'm sorry." Never demand forgiveness but definitely request it. Your spouse may need some time before offering forgiveness, and that is okay. Give them some space as they process their pain and your apology.

Let's TALK about It

Discuss the following questions together, today or throughout the week.

- What are some of the major roadblocks on the path to forgiveness?
- Has seeking forgiveness from each other gotten easier or harder the longer we've been married?
- Can we each admit a time when we asked forgiveness too quickly just to get it over with?
- Have those times become less frequent?

Let's DO Something about It

This activity may not be easy, but it is simple.

Ask your spouse, "Is there any offense I need to ask your forgiveness for?"

If so, craft an apology for what you said or did. This is key. Do not apologize for your spouse's feelings, reactions, or offense. Apologize only for your words and actions.

Let's PRAY about It

Prioritizing prayer will bring you closer together and pave the way for God to work in your life and relationship. Use the following prayer as a jumping-off point.

Father, we love and forgive because you first loved and forgave us. We forgive because we do not want you to withhold forgiveness from us. We do not want to use each other as the source of forgiveness but to receive it from you to share with one another. Let us forgive as you forgive us in Christ Jesus. We walk in the forgiveness of sins and need to be reminded of it daily so that we may in turn offer it daily as well. We praise you for your love for us. In Jesus' name. Amen.

KNOW YOUR SOURCE

If anyone acknowledges that Jesus is the Son of God, God
lives in them and they in God. And so we know and
rely on the love God has for us. God is love. Whoever
lives in love lives in God, and God in them.

1 John 4:15–16

Imagine your heart as a one-gallon milk jug. Your time with God is like water filling up the jug. Every prayer prayed, Bible passage read, worship song sung, verse memorized, and sermon heard is water in the jug. Your goal is to be as full of God's love as possible at the beginning of every day.

Throughout the day, you pour yourself out into your spouse, children, parents, strangers, friends, cashiers, tellers, servers, and drivers. Most of the time, it feels as though they take from your jug and rarely refill. That's to be expected.

It's codependency that pours into others expecting them to pour back into you. This is a terrible strategy for the joy-filled life. Why? People, places, and things cannot be your source of life. Your source of life must be Jesus, not other people—including your spouse.

Life on empty is irritable, demanding, controlling, and manipulative. We lean on people, places, or things to fill us, and when they don't, we spew. We blame others for our emptiness and demand they do something about it.

Have you ever met a clingy person? They demand your time, affirmation, and validation. They come over uninvited and stay way longer than they should. This is why Proverbs 25:17 exhorts, "Seldom set foot in your neighbor's house—too much of you, and they will hate you." Clingy people wear us out and suck the life out of us. They cling to us in hopes of receiving something they should first turn to God for: life! He, not you, must be their source.

When exhaustion and the blame game creep into our home, we have learned to say, "Jesus is my source, not you." People are limited supplies. Jesus is an unlimited supply. Imagine if two limited supplies were connected to each other, each trying to make the other their source. It doesn't work. It creates a stagnant, shallow reserve. It's nasty. No one wants to drink from that milk jug.

If that's your marriage, fire each other as the source of life. Do it right now. Point to each other and say, "You're fired!" Stop blaming each other. Plug into the true and only source of life. The best kind of marriage on the planet is one with a husband and wife connected to Jesus and filled by him. They spend their days giving each other the overflow.

By the way, it takes only one of you to get this started. No need to wait for your spouse to fire you. You fire first! Take personal responsibility for your life and heart, and plug into Jesus.

In John 6:35, Jesus said to the people, "I am the bread of life; whoever comes to me shall not hunger, and whoever believes in me shall never thirst" (ESV). He gives and sustains life. He wants to fill you so you can live a full life for him. Always stay connected to Jesus. He will never stop pouring into you.

Let's TALK about It

Discuss the following questions together, today or throughout the week.

- The last time your spouse bumped into you and upset your "milk jug," what flowed out of your heart?
- What happens to our hearts when we try to make people, places, or things the source of life?
- How do you respond to others when your heart (the milk jug) is empty?
- Can you think of a time when you ran on empty for a long time?
- What did that season of your life look like?
- When you feel drained, what do you do to be filled up with the unlimited supply of God's love?

Let's DO Something about It

At your kitchen or dining room table, gather as a couple or family for a love-jug illustration.

Bring to the table a large water pitcher or jug and an assortment of glasses and mugs (all different shapes and sizes). Assign names of children, parents, family members, friends, and coworkers to the glasses and mugs.

With a full pitcher or jug representing a heart full of God's love, start pouring into the glasses and mugs. Comment on the amount going into each. After a few pours, mention the amount left in the pitcher or jug. Have some fun with it. You may have a coworker who drains you, and yet you still fill that person's glass to the rim.

After the pouring and with a near-empty pitcher or jug, discuss as a couple or family what steps or spiritual habits keep us connected to the true and only source of life for those unlimited refills.

Let's PRAY about It

Prioritizing prayer will bring you closer together and pave the way for God to work in your life and relationship. Use the following prayer as a jumping-off point.

Father, we know and rely on you as our source of life. Fill us, not so we can be spiritual gluttons but so we can pour into others. Give us everything we need to meet the needs of others. Guard our hearts from plugging into people, places, or things as our source of life. You are our only source and always will be. In Jesus' name. Amen.

KNOW YOUR ENEMY

The thief comes only to steal and kill and destroy; I have come that they may have life, and have it to the full.

John 10:10

Your marriage has an enemy, and it is not your spouse.

Jesus is your source. Satan is your enemy. If you want to experience greater joy together, never treat your spouse as the source *or* the enemy.

God gave you your spouse to walk side by side through life together. When you walk together in Christ, you stand "strong in the Lord and in his mighty power" (Eph. 6:10).

As a couple, you do not fight your battles alone. The Lord goes before you and fights for you. Make him your source and "put on the full armor of God, so that you can take your stand against the devil's schemes" (Eph. 6:11). Satan hates you, your marriage, your family, and your church, and he will stop at nothing to take you out. He schemes to bring you down. Know your enemy so you can take your stand against him.

Satan is real. He's not wearing a red suit and holding a pitchfork. That is folk theology. He is "more crafty than any of the wild animals the LORD God had made" (Gen. 3:1). He is the "the prince of demons" (Matt. 12:24) who "has blinded the minds of unbelievers" (2 Cor. 4:4). The whole world is led astray by him (Rev. 12:9) because "he is a liar and the father of lies" (John 8:44). "The whole world is under the control of the evil one" (1 John 5:19).

Satan is brilliant. His schemes really do work. Therefore, "Be alert and of sober mind. Your enemy the devil prowls around like a roaring lion looking for someone to devour" (1 Pet. 5:8).

He is sneaky, and we often fall for his crafty ways. He uses people who don't know they're being used. And yet, our battle is not with humans but demonic beings working through them. "For our struggle is not against flesh and blood, but against the rulers, against the authorities, against the powers of this dark world and against the spiritual forces of evil in the heavenly realms" (Eph. 6:12).

People are not the enemy. You are not the enemy. Your spouse is not the enemy. Satan is the enemy.

What should we do when the attacks hit us, our marriage, and our family?

Start by standing. Paul says in Ephesians 6, "Therefore put on the full armor of God, so that when the day of evil comes, you may be able to stand your ground, and after you have done everything, to stand" (v. 13). We are called to be battle-ready at all times. Notice that the verse does not say, "When the day of evil comes, put on the full armor of God." No. It tells us to be prepared—to have the armor on already—so that when it comes, we may stand. Too many couples today are not prepared when evil strikes their marriage.

Paul tells us to stand ready with the belt of truth, the breastplate of righteousness, our feet fitted with readiness, the shield of faith, the helmet of salvation, and the sword of the Spirit.

Elsewhere, Paul tells us, "The Spirit clearly says that in later times some will abandon the faith and follow deceiving spirits and things taught by demons" (1 Tim. 4:1). How could believers do this? Because they were not wearing the full armor of God, ready for spiritual warfare.

Prayer is essential for the effectiveness of the armor. Paul ends his section on the full armor of God by emphasizing the need for prayer: "And pray in the Spirit on all occasions with all kinds of prayers and requests. With this in mind, be alert and always keep on praying for all the Lord's people" (Eph. 6:18).

Rest assured, we pray and take our stand from the position *of* victory, not one in which we're hoping *for* victory. The Bible is clear that in the end we win: "And the devil, who deceived them, was thrown into the lake of burning sulfur, where the beast and the false prophet had been thrown. They will be tormented day and night for ever and ever" (Rev. 20:10).

Let's TALK about It

Discuss the following questions together, today or throughout the week.

- What are some ways Satan might use people to carry out his schemes?
- We know how lions sneak up on their prey. Can you recount a time you were caught off guard by an evil scheme?
- What do we need to do to be prepared for battle?

Let's DO Something about It

Fire your spouse as the enemy. Like exchanging vows at your wedding, commit today to no longer view your spouse as the one against you. Repeat to your spouse the following:

I, _____*(your name)*_____, commit to you,

_____*(spouse's name)*_____, to never see you as

the enemy of me or our marriage. I promise to stand
with you against Satan and all that he throws at our
marriage.

Let's PRAY about It

Prioritizing prayer will bring you closer together and pave the way for
God to work in your life and relationship. Use the following prayer as
a jumping-off point.

*Father, deliver us from evil. Fill our minds with your Word. We ask that
the Holy Spirit recall to our hearts and minds your words when we are
tempted or when we accuse each other in our struggles. We do not want
to look at each other as the enemy but to know the true enemy of our
marriage and take our stand against him. We understand that in every
moment of temptation, you alone have the power to deliver us from it. We
praise you for your power. In Jesus' name we pray. Amen.*

KNOW YOURSELF

Each of you should use whatever gift you have received to serve others, as faithful stewards of God's grace in its various forms.

1 Peter 4:10

The Chicago Cubs are ahead 14–1 in the top of the ninth. Relief pitcher David Robertson steps up to bat—not pitch—for the very first time in his fourteen years in the majors. This is his 696th game and his first at bat.

Pitchers are not great batters. This is common knowledge. No one expects them to hit well. After all, their job is to throw strikes. They train with pitching coaches, not batting coaches.

Robertson steps up to the plate with the biggest smile on his face. The entire Cubs dugout is on their feet cheering for him. Even the fans of the opposing team cheer for him. This is a big moment, one that David would not waste.

Diego Castillo, pitching for the Pittsburgh Pirates, was rooting for Robertson too. Like they were playing softball, he lobbed his pitches in at 40 mph. But Robertson still struck out. With each swing and consecutive miss, the smile on Robertson's face beamed brighter. There was no rejection in his walk back to the dugout. He walked back to high fives and cheers as if he'd just hit a grand slam. No one expected a home run because he was a pitcher.

There is great relief and joy in knowing who you are and what God has called you to do in life. There will always be someone who is smarter, faster, stronger, and better than you. Comparison is a joy killer.

> Each of you should use whatever gift you have received to serve others, as faithful stewards of God's grace in its various forms. If anyone speaks, they should do so as one who speaks the very words of God. If anyone serves, they should do so with the strength God provides, so that in all things God may be praised through Jesus Christ. To him be the glory and the power for ever and ever. Amen. (1 Pet. 4:10–11)

We serve God and others best when we know the spiritual gifts God has given each one of us and use them to serve others. Since I appreciate how God wired Amy, I walk alongside her to help her use the gifts he placed within her. Recognizing her spiritual wiring gives me greater opportunity to acknowledge and amplify her value and service.

Using God's gifts in his power brings glory to him. I do not rely on my own strength and my own way, and I do not work for my own glory. We want our marriage and service to others to bring praise to the Father. He deserves all the glory.

There is a caution that accompanies us zeroing in on our gifts and calling in life. When we find our sweet spot in serving the Lord, there are no more excuses for not using our gifts—or improving them. I am not a pitcher, so I don't train for pitching. I am a teacher with twenty-five years' experience. Time, training, practice, and experience make people better at their calling.

However, depending on the spiritual gift we've been given, if we are not careful, we can become filled with entitlement and spiritual pride. Jesus knew this and gave us this warning:

> Suppose one of you has a servant plowing or looking after the sheep. Will he say to the servant when he comes in from the field, "Come along now and sit down to eat"? Won't he rather say, "Prepare my supper, get yourself ready and wait on me while I eat and drink; after that you may eat and drink"? Will he thank the servant because he did what he was told to do? So you also, when you have done everything you were told to do, should say, "We are unworthy servants; we have only done our duty." (Luke 17:7–10)

Keep serving. Stay humble. You and I are unworthy servants serving a great God. Do not let your head swell. Know your calling and gifts. Lean into them and Jesus together. Rest in who God made you to be and what he has called you to do.

Let's TALK about It

Discuss the following questions together, today or throughout the week.

- Do you know your spiritual gifts? Can you name them?
- Would you be open to taking an online spiritual gifts assessment in an effort to home in on them? If so, do an internet search for one and take it.

- Have you ever had someone reject or take advantage of your spiritual service? Did it make you want to stop serving?
- What is one way I serve you each week that you appreciate the most?

Let's DO Something about It

Here's a fun and quick exercise.

Find a video on YouTube about Chicago Cubs pitcher David Robertson batting.

Discuss your observations and takeaways from that clip. (Like a good FBI training video, there is much in it to observe.)

Let's PRAY about It

Prioritizing prayer will bring you closer together and pave the way for God to work in your life and relationship. Use the following prayer as a jumping-off point.

Father, help us to never compare what you have for us to do against what you have given someone else to do. Keep us in our lane, focused on the finish line ahead of us. As others pass us in their lane, give us the heart to cheer them on. As believers in you, we are all on the same team. We want all our gifts and service this week to glorify you. You are worthy of all our praise! It is in the mighty and wonderful name of Jesus that we ask these things. Amen!

A STRONG FOUNDATION

The rain came down, the streams rose, and the winds
blew and beat against that house; yet it did not fall,
because it had its foundation on the rock.

Matthew 7:25

We live in Missouri, and our house is built on limestone. It's a soft rock that expands and contracts with the changing seasons. We have the cracks in our walls to prove it. My daughter's room has one about three feet long that comes and goes each summer.

I "drywall mudded" it the first few years but eventually gave up. Experts tell me there's a simple fix we can make in our crawl space to shore up the foundation, but we have not taken those steps. Our house won't collapse anytime soon. We choose to fix the cracks cosmetically.

What a great illustration of a fractured marriage. There are cracks there, but they are hidden by a little drywall mud. The casual observer will never see those cracks. The couple may not crash or end their marriage, but the brokenness is there.

Every marriage is built on something. Some are built on attraction, careers, kids, or wealth. Those couples' foundation shudders when looks fade, jobs are lost, the kids leave home, or the stock market crashes. But there is a better way.

Every marriage goes through storms. We do not choose everything that happens to us in life, but we do choose what we build our marriage upon. Jesus refers to this as the foundation:

> Therefore everyone who hears these words of mine and *puts them into practice* is like a wise man who built his house on the rock. The rain came down, the streams rose, and the winds blew and beat against that house; yet it did not fall, because it had its foundation on the rock. But everyone who hears these words of mine and *does not put them into practice* is like a foolish man who built his house on sand. The rain came down, the streams rose, and the winds blew and beat against that house, and it fell with a great crash. (Matt. 7:24–27)

From the curb, these houses look identical. The storms that hit them are the same. There's one major difference: the foundation.

Some blame the storm for the great crash. They say, "It was just too much for the couple to endure. The loss of a child, their health, the job, or their home. Their marriage did not make it because the storm crushed them."

But the truth is that the cause was the foundation, not the storm. Storms *reveal* foundations. You do not crash because of the storms. You crash because of a weak foundation.

Have you ever met a seasoned believer who was steady and secure? Their steadiness is not because their life was easy. Their steadfastness is found in their foundation. No matter what hits their life or marriage, they stand. That is the power of the Word of God.

You do not crash because of the storms. You crash because of a weak foundation.

Your foundation is determined by what you do with the Word of God, not by what you know *about* the Word of God. Both builders heard the words of Jesus, but only one put them into practice. Jesus said, "Now that you know these things, you will be blessed if you do them" (John 13:17).

Do not wait for a storm before you decide to work on your foundation. If you have recently experienced a great crash, work on your foundation before rebuilding. A strong foundation secures your marriage when storms rage.

Let's TALK about It

Discuss the following questions together, today or throughout the week.

- What is the greatest storm to ever hit our marriage?
- Did it feel like we were going to crash?
- What significant faith decisions did we make after that storm passed?
- Do we know of other couples who have experienced a similar storm?
- What did we learn from watching them go through it?
- If we are not careful, what weak foundation could we easily build on instead of the Word of God?

Let's DO Something about It

Let's work on our foundation. For the next seven days, let's take a few minutes each day to read together the following passages on the power and life found in God's Word.

Day 1—Psalm 1:1–3; Psalm 119:105
Day 2—Psalm 119:11; Joshua 1:8
Day 3—Matthew 24:35; Isaiah 40:8
Day 4—2 Timothy 2:15; Colossians 3:16
Day 5—James 1:23–25; 1 Thessalonians 2:13
Day 6—1 Peter 2:2–3; Jeremiah 20:8–9
Day 7—Hebrews 4:12; 2 Timothy 3:16–17

Let's PRAY about It

Prioritizing prayer will bring you closer together and pave the way for God to work in your life and relationship. Use the following prayer as a jumping-off point.

Jesus, your Word is our firm foundation. May we never build on emotion, experience, reason, or tradition. Let each storm give us pause to open our Bibles and hear from you. Your words are life and power for our marriage. They light our path and keep us from crashing. Thank you for giving us the gift of your Word. We praise you for it. In Jesus' name. Amen.

MEMORIZE AND MEDITATE

For the word of God is alive and active. Sharper than any double-edged sword, it penetrates even to dividing soul and spirit, joints and marrow; it judges the thoughts and attitudes of the heart.

Hebrews 4:12

God has blessed me with many great mentors, both in life and ministry. They all walked beside me early in ministry and gave me a hunger for God's Word. Not only did they preach the Bible, but they also passionately pursued the spiritual disciplines of memorizing and meditating on it. They believed this was a key to faithful, effective ministry.

More than twenty years ago, one of our church elders planted two willow trees by a pond near his home. Both trees were identical in size when planted. Years later, one tree was twice as big as the other. The stark difference between the two trees caught my eye every time I drove by the pond.

Why was one doing so well and the other lagging behind? When you walked closer to the trees, the explanation was plain to see: The larger tree was planted closer to the pond than the other. Their proximity to the pond determined their health and size. What a powerful word picture.

Psalm 1:1–3 uses the image of a tree planted by water to help us understand the life of one who sets down roots in the Scripture:

> Blessed is the one
>   who does not walk in step with the wicked
> or stand in the way that sinners take
>   or sit in the company of mockers,
> but whose delight is in the law of the LORD,
>   and who meditates on his law day and night.
> That person is like a tree planted by streams of water,
>   which yields its fruit in season
> and whose leaf does not wither—
>   whatever they do prospers.

Trees need water to survive and thrive. You and I are like those trees, and God's Word is the water. Memorizing and meditating on Scripture keeps us connected to the true and only source of life.

There are many simple and helpful ways to memorize Scripture. First, you can memorize passages of Scripture with your family. Set a goal to memorize a new verse or passage together every week. Revisit the passages daily as you "talk about them when you sit at home and when you walk along the road, when you lie down and when you get up" (Deut. 6:7).

Second, write verses out on index cards or sticky notes. Place them on mirrors, computers, and other prominent places around the house, office, and car. One of the keys to memorization is keeping the text in front of you.

Third, use downtime to memorize. Instead of mindlessly surfing social media while in lines, drive-throughs, or waiting rooms, or before the start of a meeting, use that time to pull out your cards and go over a verse a few more times. This is one reason I love the Bible App. It's on my phone and with me everywhere I go. Those waiting moments become great opportunities for memorizing.

Once a verse finds its way into your heart, the Holy Spirit recalls it for you when you need it: when you're facing temptation, for example, or sharing your faith or counseling a couple. Committing Scripture to memory is like expanding the Holy Spirit's ready vocabulary in your mind.

One of my greatest joys as a pastor is pointing out some of the lies people believe about God, themselves, and others. For example, if I am meeting with someone who feels worthless and that idea keeps coming out in our conversation, I can remind them of Genesis 1:27 and the fact that they are created in the image of God. I love that I can quote the full verse by memory. The words give them automatic, intrinsic value, and I didn't even have to pause to look up the passage. The person may feel worthless, but the truth is that they are highly valuable.

Memorizing Scripture helps me detect errors and lies. The Holy Spirit prompts me with the verse, and I am able to share it at just the right moment. When I see red flags of lies from culture, the truth of God's Word comes to mind. The Scripture is "alive and active" and with us at all times. Meditating on Scripture is one of the best ways to guard your heart from toxic beliefs.

Memorizing and meditating on Scripture gives us a firm grip on "the sword of the Spirit, which is the word of God" (Eph. 6:17). It gives us everything we need for the battles we face. Make no mistake, the devil wants you to drop the sword. He wants you to stand defenseless against his lies.

I texted a mentor recently and asked him his thoughts on the importance of a life rooted in Scripture. He texted back, "Memorizing and meditating on Scripture brings intimacy with God, freedom from sin, emotional peace to the heart, and rest to the weary soul."

What a great reminder for each of us to continue in this spiritual discipline.

Let's TALK about It

Discuss the following questions together, today or throughout the week.

- How does memorizing and meditating on Scripture help a believer grow?
- What is the first verse you memorized as a new believer?
- When was the last time the Holy Spirit brought a verse to your mind?
- What was the verse, and how did it apply to your situation?

Let's DO Something about It

- Memorize and meditate as a couple on 2 Timothy 3:16–17 this week: "All Scripture is God-breathed and is useful for teaching, rebuking, correcting and training in righteousness, so that the servant of God may be thoroughly equipped for every good work."
- Meditate on a passage of Scripture that you have read or heard preached recently that taught you something new.

- When was the last time the Scripture corrected or rebuked you?
- How did memorizing and meditating on 2 Timothy 3:16–17 grow your faith in Christ this week?

Let's PRAY about It

Prioritizing prayer will bring you closer together and pave the way for God to work in your life and relationship. Use the following prayer as a jumping-off point.

Lord, your Word is a lamp unto my feet and a light unto my path. Teach us. Rebuke us. Correct us. Train us in righteousness. You have good works for us to do, and we want to be ready for them. Plant us in your Word like trees by living water. Grow us closer to you as we spend time in your Word together. We thank you for giving us the gift of your Word. We praise you for it. In Jesus' name. Amen.

Week 37

EARN, GIVE, SAVE, SPEND

*No one can serve two masters. Either you will hate the one
and love the other, or you will be devoted to the one and
despise the other. You cannot serve both God and money.*

Matthew 6:24

Money is not the root of all evil. The *love* of money is the root of all evil.

Amy and I never want money to rule or consume our marriage. Few things drain the joy out of marriage faster than the constant struggle and conflict that come from bad money habits.

We follow one simple money formula: earn, give, save, and spend—in that order. This order keeps us from serving money.

From as early as I can remember, my dad taught my brother and me this formula. When we earned money from mowing yards, raking leaves, or digging ditches around the neighborhood, we brought it home, and Dad helped us break it down. The tithe was first—10 percent right off the top. After setting some aside for missions too, about 50 percent went into savings. The rest was ours to spend wisely.

It all starts with earning. Inspired by Dave Ramsey, I love asking my kids, "Where do you go when you want money?"

Then we all yell, "You go to work."

According to Proverbs, hunger is a great motivator to work. If you want to eat, you must work. If you refuse to work, you will starve:

> There is a way that appears to be right,
>   but in the end it leads to death.
> The appetite of laborers works for them;
>   their hunger drives them on. (16:25–26)

Diligent workers find contentment in their labor. When people stay busy and productive, they have very little time to complain or whine about life "because God keeps them occupied with gladness of heart" (Eccl. 5:20).

Giving should be the very first thought after earning. Giving is our automatic response of thanksgiving to the One who enabled us to work. God's call is to "honor the LORD with your wealth, with the firstfruits of all your crops" (Prov. 3:9). When you get paid, your first question should be, "What can I give?" not, "What can I get?" Giving reminds you that you are a steward, not an owner. Give cheerfully, "not reluctantly or under compulsion, for God loves a cheerful giver" (2 Cor. 9:7). Give quietly: "Then your Father, who sees what is done in secret, will reward you" (Matt. 6:4).

After you earn and give, next comes saving. The fool spends everything he makes: "The wise store up choice food and olive oil, but fools gulp theirs down" (Prov. 21:20). Make sure something goes in the bank before you go shopping online. Build up an emergency fund so you are not caught off guard by some sudden cost for car or home repairs. Use your prime earning years to put something away for when you will not be able to work as much. Money grows over time and "whoever gathers money little by little makes it grow" (Prov. 13:11). Save something, even if it does not feel like much.

After you earn, give, and save, spend the remaining balance on your personal and household budget. We are consumers, but we could do a better job of reeling in our spending. Some spend out of entitlement. They confuse privilege for necessity by feeling they deserve something. Some are emotional spenders, making purchases to medicate pain, hurt, or loss. Others are essential spenders and get by with the basics.

Consume less to enjoy more. Budget for contentment. Like the apostle Paul, may we learn "to be content whatever the circumstances" (Phil. 4:11). Avoid debt whenever possible because "the rich rule over the poor, and the borrower is slave to the lender" (Prov. 22:7). If your spending is out of control, take a look at your giving. When we prioritize generosity over consumption, our spending tends to keep in check with our budget.

I know a lot of couples who hate talking about money. One of the reasons this is such a painful conversation is because of the embarrassment accompanying our mismanaged finances. Get your house and accounts in order with the simple "earn, give, save, spend" formula. Greater joy awaits every couple who stops serving money and turns to the One who owns it all.

Let's TALK about It

Discuss the following questions together, today or throughout the week.

- Are you happy with the current state of our finances?
- Does our money management follow the "earn, give, save, spend" formula?
- Do we need to do more earning, giving, saving, or spending? Where do you want to start? What would be your goal?

- Has there ever been a time when our spending was so out of control that it kept us from giving and saving?
- What can we cut to keep our spending under control?

Let's DO Something about It

Below is a simple, sample monthly budget to open the conversation about your earning, giving, saving, and spending. If you really want to get serious, transfer this to a spreadsheet or app to better track your finances. Feel free to round off amounts for the sake of time and conversation.

Earning (our monthly take-home pay): _____

Giving:
    Tithe (10% of gross income) _____
    Extra offering _____
    Ministries/Missions support _____

Saving:
    Retirement plan _____
    Savings account _____

Spending:
    Mortgage/Rent _____
    Utilities _____
    Food _____
    Transportation _____
    Insurance _____
    Debt payments _____
    School expenses _____

Household maintenance/services _____

Entertainment _____

Other _____

Total giving, saving, spending: _____

Balance remaining formula:

Earning − (Giving + Saving + Spending) =

_____

Let's PRAY about It

Prioritizing prayer will bring you closer together and pave the way for God to work in your life and relationship. Use the following prayer as a jumping-off point.

Lord, we are stewards of everything you give us. You are our provider and sustainer. We thank you for our work and all that it provides us. We're so grateful for the opportunity to care for the needs of others. May our generosity reflect yours. We serve you, not money. In Jesus' name. Amen.

Week 38

THE JOY OF WORK

To enjoy your work and accept your lot in
life—this is indeed a gift from God.
Ecclesiastes 5:19 NLT

"If you love your job, you'll never work a day in your life."

Have you ever heard someone say that? It usually refers to the type of work you do. If you love it, supposedly it won't ever feel burdensome. However, the Bible stresses that our attitude at work is far more important than the type of work we do.

Scripture gives us several motives for work. Just as we find joy in a spouse's activity because we are doing that activity for them, so we find joy in our jobs because we are doing it for the Lord.

We work for the Lord. "Whatever you do, work at it with all your heart, as working for the Lord, not for human masters" (Col. 3:23). The pep talk I gave my kids before dropping them off for babysitting gigs or their first job at the candy store was "Give it everything. Your ultimate boss is the Lord. Give 100 percent, have a great attitude, show up on time, and don't quit early." Cheating the time clock, stealing from work, or having a bad attitude toward customers is between you and the Lord, not you and your boss. We present our labor to the Lord to glorify him.

We work for food. "The appetite of laborers works for them; their hunger drives them on" (Prov. 16:26). Years ago, two young men in our community chatted on Facebook about their lack of funds for rent and food. The one guy, who didn't have a job, shared with his buddy, "I don't have enough money to cover rent this month. I'm thinking about starting a GoFundMe page to see if I can get some people to help me out."

His friend responded, "You should call Woodland Hills Church. They help people like us."

There was no need for me to comment on this dialogue on Facebook because a church member beat me to it. He simply replied in the comments, "NOPE!"

I wanted to add, "You don't need a fundraiser or a gift from the benevolence fund—you need a job." I refrained.

We work for our family. My joy in life is providing for my family. I love covering expenses for my family members and making sure Amy has plenty of money to get what she and our family need.

Part of adulthood is providing for someone other than yourself. Paul was clear: "Anyone who does not provide for their relatives, and especially for their own household, has denied the faith and is worse than an unbeliever" (1 Tim. 5:8).

We work for our future needs. More than an emergency fund, you need funds to cover the time when you won't be able to work as much. When I work, I think about the current and future needs of our family. Proverbs calls this wisdom: "He who gathers crops in summer is a prudent son, but he who sleeps during harvest is a disgraceful son." (10:5).

We also work for the needs our family will have after we are dead and gone. Proverbs 13:22 declares, "A good person leaves an inheritance for their children's children."

We work to be generous. This one keeps me from thinking about retiring. I love working so that I may be even more generous. Paul challenged the believers in Ephesus to work and do "something useful with their own hands, that they may have something to share with those in need" (Eph. 4:28).

Jesus gives us breath and strength to work and provide for our families, future, and the needs of others. You may need to get a new job that better fits your giftedness, skills, and experience. Either way, serve Jesus and others with a great attitude.

Let's TALK about It

Discuss the following questions together, today or throughout the week.

- What was your first job?
- How much did you make?
- What was your worst job as a teenager?
- What was your favorite job as a teenager?
- Do you enjoy your current job? If not, why?
- Is there anything you can change about your mindset to enjoy your current job more?

Let's DO Something about It

Marriage is a great asset, not a hindrance, to our work. We lean on each other for strength, prayer, and replenishment during and at the end of a long workday. Make a list of your greatest challenges at work.

Two ways to use this list:

1. Pray specifically for each other.
2. Follow up with each other after work.

His Challenges at Work	Her Challenges at Work
_____	_____
_____	_____
_____	_____
_____	_____
_____	_____
_____	_____
_____	_____

Let's PRAY about It

Prioritizing prayer will bring you closer together and pave the way for God to work in your life and relationship. Use the following prayer as a jumping-off point.

Lord, our work is worship. You gave us knowledge, skills, and strength to make money and provide for the needs of each other, our family, and others. You alone are our ultimate boss. We want our work to be pleasing to you. Thank you for our jobs. We want to exhibit Christlike attitudes in our work each day. In Jesus' name we pray. Amen.

Week 39

THE JOY OF GIVING

One person gives freely, yet gains even more;
another withholds unduly, but comes to poverty.
A generous person will prosper;
whoever refreshes others will be refreshed.

Proverbs 11:24–25

The most generous people I know give away blessings, gifts, and resources as quickly as possible. The secret to joy and success is to not hoard the blessings we receive from God. When we receive a gift, our first thought should be, "Who can I bless with this?"

Amy and I have a dear friend who refuses to spend gift cards. When he receives one, he immediately finds someone who needs it more than he does or someone who could use the encouragement. (This is meant to inspire you, not guilt you.) There's nothing wrong with taking a gift card and allowing the giver to be blessed in their giving. But when blessings come my way I want my first thought to be, "How can I bless someone else with this?" A generous giver receives from the Lord and seeks opportunities to bless others.

God's blessings do not stop when they reach us—they fuel us for every good work. We want God's blessings to flow through us. Paul reminds us that "God is able to bless you abundantly, so that in all things at all times, having all that you need, you will abound in every good work" (2 Cor. 9:8).

God's people should be known as the most generous people on the planet. A stingy Christian is an oxymoron.

Stingy people look away from opportunities. Stingy people are consciously unaware of needs around them, and they try to avoid needs when they present themselves. Proverbs 28:27 says, "Those who give to the poor will lack nothing, but those who close their eyes to them receive many curses." We have all done this. We avoid eye contact with the panhandler or the stranger in need. But generous people keep their head on a swivel and are always on the lookout for ways to help others.

Stingy people delay when they see need. Proverbs 3:27–28 says, "Do not withhold good from those to whom it is due, when it is in your power to act. Do not say to your neighbor, 'Come back tomorrow and I'll give it to you'—when you already have it with you." Do you have generous people in your life? Generous people are quick to respond to need. Stingy people make excuses.

I know that someone might think, *I don't have enough money to be generous,* or *If I came into a million bucks, I'd be generous.* Your generosity is determined by your character and commitment to the Lord, not by your paycheck, bank account, or financial windfall. Income determines your capacity, not your generosity.

Jesus told the story of the widow's mite to draw the line between heart motivation and capacity. He is concerned with your heart, not your net worth.

> As Jesus looked up, he saw the rich putting their gifts
> into the temple treasury. He also saw a poor widow

put in two very small copper coins. "Truly I tell you," he said, "this poor widow has put in more than all the others. All these people gave their gifts out of their wealth; but she out of her poverty put in all she had to live on." (Luke 21:1–4)

Generosity is for the poor and the rich. I know people making $50,000 a year who are far more generous than some making seven figures. God wants cheerful and sacrificial giving. And let us not forget: God does not need our money—he wants our hearts.

For this reason, Paul instructed Timothy to implore the rich to not be consumed with their wealth: "Command them to do good, to be rich in good deeds, and to be generous and willing to share. In this way they will lay up treasure for themselves as a firm foundation for the coming age, so that they may take hold of the life that is truly life" (1 Tim. 6:18–19).

Income determines your capacity, not your generosity.

Scripture says that when the church was formed in the first century, "God's grace was so powerfully at work in them all" (Acts 4:33). God's grace was so powerfully at work in them because of their love for him, and their generosity was one outcome of their love. "All the believers were one in heart and mind. No one claimed that any of their possessions was their own, but they shared everything they had" (Acts 4:32).

Surround yourself with generous people. Join a generous church. Look for opportunities to pass your blessings on to others. Never claim your possessions as your own. After all, we are stewards, not owners, of all that God provides.

Let's TALK about It

Discuss the following questions together, today or throughout the week.

- Is your first thought *Whom can I bless with this?* when you are blessed?
- Is either one of us holding the other back from acts of generosity?
- What keeps us from responding immediately to needs?
- When has our capacity held us back from generosity?
- What are your thoughts on tithing (giving 10 percent of income to the local church)?

Let's DO Something about It

Take the initiative this week to perform a random act of generosity. Think of an individual or couple you want to bless. What is their favorite restaurant in town? Buy a gift card for that restaurant in an amount that buys their meal. Again, capacity is not the focus. It can be Chick-fil-A, Red Lobster, or a Michelin-star restaurant. Bless that couple as quietly as possible.

Let's PRAY about It

Prioritizing prayer will bring you closer together and pave the way for God to work in your life and relationship. Use the following prayer as a jumping-off point.

Father, in the name of Jesus, we want to be a generous couple. Jesus modeled this when he gave his life for us. We never want to be marked as stingy or sowing sparingly. Give us eyes to see needs. May we continue to give and meet the needs. Generosity reminds us that we are stewards, not owners. It is all yours. We will be wise stewards and generous givers. We pray these things in the wonderful and powerful name of Jesus. Amen.

Week 40

MORE JOY IN WHAT YOU HAVE

But if we have food and clothing, we
will be content with that.

1 Timothy 6:8

Amy and I call them *clicks*. We do the majority of our shopping online. No more trips to the mall or waiting at the checkout. We search for it in seconds, have it in the cart within minutes, and it is on our front step in a day or two. Each item is a click. We ask each other in jest at the end of the day, "So, how many clicks today?"

The convenience of it all challenges our contentment daily. And around the holidays or when we're preparing for vacation, spending fatigue sets in.

Paul warned Timothy and the believers in Ephesus of the snare that keeps us from enjoying what we have in hand.

> But if we have food and clothing, we will be content with that. Those who want to get rich fall into temptation and a trap and into many foolish and harmful desires that plunge people into ruin and destruction. For the love of money is a root of all kinds of evil. Some people,

eager for money, have wandered from the faith and pierced themselves with many griefs. (1 Tim. 6:8–10)

Did you catch that? Money is not the root of all evil. The *love* of money is.

A few years ago, Amy and I compiled a list of practical ways to curb our appetite for stuff. It helps us find contentment when the clicks are out of control. Maybe it will help you avoid some of the grievances that come with the love of money.

1. **Make a list of things we want but don't need.** On my list is a snorkel for my truck. Will my truck ever cross a creek or river so deep that I'd need a snorkel for it? Probably not. That will remain on my list until the Lord returns.

2. **See how long you can make something last.** We once gave out O'Reilly Auto Parts gift cards to the person in each church service with the most miles on their current vehicle. One guy had over 480,000 miles on his Toyota Tacoma, which received a collective gasp from the congregation. Since I drive a Tacoma too, it gave me something to aim for.

3. **Deny yourself something you could easily afford.** This is discipline. My dad drives a Ford Taurus. He could afford to get the air-conditioning fixed, but he chooses not to. For me, that rides the line between discipline and insanity, but it works for him.

4. **Refuse to be defined by brands.** Growing up, Levi's were for kids with wealthy parents. We were middle class, so we wore Lee jeans. No one

bragged about Lee jeans. Enjoy your nice purse or shoes, but do not let them define you.

5. **Unsubscribe from daily retail emails that spike your want-o-meter.** Advertising has one main goal: to make us feel discontent so we crave their stuff. Unsubscribing from Pottery Barn, William Sonoma, and Bass Pro keeps me from knowing (and yearning for) what I am missing.

6. **Take your time with large purchases.** Eliminate impulse buying. Take your time and shop around when you're looking at big appliances, furniture, and vehicles. We live in a day when a click can get you a car delivered to your driveway. The convenience is great, but do your research first.

7. **Plan on emergencies.** After you earn and give, get that emergency account going. Have some money set aside so you do not have to be stressed when the car breaks down or the HVAC unit needs to be replaced.

Contentment gives us peace. Discontentment steals our joy. We sleep at night knowing the basics for our family are met. We also know that every square inch we own owns us. The more we have, the more we have to take care of. Couples grateful for what they have find greater joy in life and marriage.

Let's TALK about It

Discuss the following questions together, today or throughout the week.

- List a few things you want but don't need.
- What is the last purchase you regretted?

- What do we own now that takes too much time and maintenance to keep?
- Why don't we get rid of it?

Let's DO Something about It

Consider a one-week spending fast. Agree upon a "no-spend list." For example, no online purchases for the next seven days or no eating out for seven days. Make the list your own. The terms must be mutually agreed upon. At the end of the week, discuss the following questions:

- How painful was that?
- Did you feel like you were missing out?
- Is this something you could see us doing often?
- Would you consider a spending fast for a few weeks or a month?
- What should we do with the money we saved this past week?

Let's PRAY about It

Prioritizing prayer will bring you closer together and pave the way for God to work in your life and relationship. Use the following prayer as a jumping-off point.

Father, we serve you, not money. We never want money to stand in the way of our relationship with you. Let us use money to bless others. Faithfulness and stewardship are our goals. Thank you for the breath you give us to work and earn. We receive everything we have with thanksgiving. It is in the name of Jesus that we pray. Amen.

THE GROWN-UP MARRIAGE

When I was a child, I spoke like a child, I thought
like a child, I reasoned like a child. When I
became a man, I gave up childish ways.

1 Corinthians 13:11 ESV

Have you ever tried to reason with a toddler? It doesn't work.

Right before our son turned two, we took him on the last free flight of his lifetime. The seat next to us was empty, so he did not have to sit on our laps.

In his big-boy seat, he repeatedly kicked the seat in front of him. The guy in that seat turned around and gave me the "Take care of this" look. I used my arm to block Carson's legs from the seat back and said, "Do not kick the seat." He complied … at first.

As soon as I removed my arm, he looked over at me with a smirk on his face and kicked the seat. We were on a plane full of people, so I freaked out on the inside.

I placed my arm on his legs again and he did not resist. But when I removed my arm, he kicked again. He repeated this for several minutes. He was a child acting like a child.

We expect children to speak, think, and reason like children. Childish ways lead to tantrums and fits. When a child wants something they cannot have, all reasoning goes out the window.

Have you ever pitched a fit in your marriage? When you do not get your way, do you revert to childish reasoning?

Childish speaking and thinking emphasize *I* and *me* more than *you*, *we*, and *us*. In a maturing marriage, spouses make major decisions and enjoy activities with each other in mind. Adulting requires that we think about the other person's needs, wants, and desires—not just our own. And we not only think about them, but we also act on them.

Amy wades in the Kenai River in Alaska with me because I sit in Anthropologie with her. I watch rom-com movies with her because she watches Liam Neeson action movies with me.

A major and often-overlooked part of adulthood is finding great joy in what others enjoy—in finding *Greater Joy TWOgether*, you might say.

We reinforced this with our kids as they moved from childhood into adulthood. Parents find joy in what brings their children joy. I hate roller coasters, but my son loves them, so I love going on them for him.

Childish reasoning includes thoughts like *mine* and *now* rather than *ours*, *yours*, and *later*. Children are in the moment. Adults think about the future.

The more I work with couples, the more convinced I am that prolonged adolescence (prioritizing privilege over responsibility) is a leading cause of divorce. Seeking privilege and avoiding responsibility is part of childhood. When you prioritize responsibility over privilege, on the other hand, your character matures and your marriage thrives.

Which of the following scenarios best describes your marriage?

1. **We were mature when we married.** If the motto of your childhood homes was "Family fun when

the chores are done," then this may be how your marriage started.

2. **We were immature when we married but grew up together.** We had lingering privilege and childish ways early on, but we worked through them in our marriage.

3. **We were immature when we married; I grew up but my spouse did not.** Spouses mature at different paces. One may come into the marriage with more maturity than the other. This is common, and it requires patience and grace to grow up together.

4. **We were immature when we married; my spouse grew up but I did not.** Admitting this is a great first step to maturity.

5. **We were immature when we married, and we still are.** If this is you, there is hope. Press on. Do not quit. Use this as an opportunity to start making adulthood decisions.

My son is now seventeen and brings great joy to our family. We have deep, mature conversations about his faith, school, and relationships. I love being a parent to adult children, and I love my marriage to an adult spouse. I want to bring mature words, thoughts, and reasoning to all these relationships.

Let's TALK about It

Discuss the following questions together, today or throughout the week.

- How would you describe our maturity in the early years of our marriage?

- When did you start to really see a change in me?
- Do you ever feel like we have grown enough?
- Can you think of any couples who were mature when they married? Who? What stood out the most about their maturity?

Let's DO Something about It

List three activities that you enjoy, but you're pretty sure your spouse does not.

His Activities
1.
2.
3.

Her Activities
1.
2.
3.

Circle the activity on your spouse's list that you enjoy the least.

If you're willing, make a plan to participate this week in the activity you just circled.

Let's PRAY about It

Prioritizing prayer will bring you closer together and pave the way for God to work in your life and relationship. Use the following prayer as a jumping-off point.

Father, we press on toward maturity in you and in our marriage. We ask that the Holy Spirit convict us when childish ways surface. Call them out so that we may address them. We never want to get to a place where we say we have grown enough. We thank you for your grace, and for the opportunity to grow and mature in Jesus' name. Amen.

Week 42

THE SECRET TO A LIFE-GIVING MARRIAGE

The Son of Man did not come to be served, but to
serve, and to give his life as a ransom for many.
Matthew 20:28

Serving is the antidote for selfishness, entitlement, and pride. Jesus modeled for us the principle that serving is the greatest secret to a joy-filled, life-giving marriage.

First-century believers knew this secret, and the church thrived because of it. In Acts 2:44–45 we read: "All the believers were together and had everything in common. They sold property and possessions to give to anyone who had need." They were all together for Jesus, meeting the needs of others.

Immediately following the birth of the church, believers in Jesus radically served together to meet the needs of others. By the time we get to chapter 4 in Acts, we see this life-giving power at work among them:

> All the believers were one in heart and mind. No one claimed that any of their possessions was their own, but they shared everything they had. With great power the apostles continued to testify to the resurrection of

the Lord Jesus. And God's grace was so powerfully at work in them all that there were no needy persons among them. For from time to time those who owned land or houses sold them, brought the money from the sales and put it at the apostles' feet, and it was distributed to anyone who had need. (vv. 32–35)

Their oneness overflowed in love and ministry, and it testified to the resurrection of Jesus. When we serve one another, we testify to the life found in Jesus.

Can you imagine being married to someone who gets up every morning with a desire to serve you? What would you do if your son or daughter walked into the kitchen tomorrow morning and said, "Blessed mother, what can I do to serve you today? I know you have a lot going on, and I do not want to be a burden. Just the opposite: I want to help make your load light today." After you awoke from fainting and picked yourself up off the floor, you'd embrace the greatest child on earth.

> To be life giving like Jesus, we must give our lives in service to each other.

In June 2022, my wife sprained her ankle while decluttering our house. It was the most severe sprain I have ever seen. Her ankle swelled up and turned purple. A few days later, her entire foot and all her toes were purple. The sprain kept her from daily exercise.

Five days into recovery, she said, "I think the best thing for my ankle is a good workout. We need to walk this morning."

"Hmm," I responded with eyebrows raised, "that's not at all what the doctor said. His instructions were to stay off it, elevate, and ice."

We took it slowly but walked a mile that morning. Her grit inspired me. It also reminded me how one part of the body can keep the whole body from moving.

Paul encouraged the church in Corinth with these words: "Just as a body, though one, has many parts, but all its many parts form one body, so it is with Christ" (1 Cor. 12:12).

Just as Amy did not let her ankle hold her body back, I never want my part in the body of Christ to keep the rest of the body from moving. I want my service in life, ministry, and marriage to keep others healthy, growing, and moving. That brings life to the whole body.

In Matthew 20, Jesus teaches the disciples what serving in the kingdom looks like:

> Jesus called them together and said, "You know that the rulers of the Gentiles lord it over them, and their high officials exercise authority over them. Not so with you. Instead, whoever wants to become great among you must be your servant, and whoever wants to be first must be your slave—just as the Son of Man did not come to be served, but to serve, and to give his life as a ransom for many." (vv. 25–28)

Jesus gave his life for us. He is our model. To be life giving like Jesus, we must give our lives in service to each other. Let that service start in your marriage.

Let's TALK about It

Discuss the following questions together, today or throughout the week.

- What is the greatest or most surprising act of service someone has ever done for us as a couple?
- Thinking through the ministry of Jesus, what are some examples of how he served people?
- Share with your spouse some of the ways they serve like Jesus.

Let's DO Something about It

Take a few minutes to consider all the things that need to happen to keep your home running smoothly. Start by each writing your top three needs around the house. Then give your spouse time to interview you on those needs for better ways to serve. Take some good notes for serving ideas moving forward. You may already do plenty to serve those needs, so this could lead to a conversation of great appreciation.

Her Needs	Ways I Serve Her
_____	_____
_____	_____
_____	_____
_____	_____
_____	_____
_____	_____

His Needs	Ways I Serve Him
_____	_____
_____	_____
_____	_____
_____	_____
_____	_____
_____	_____
_____	_____
_____	_____

Let's PRAY about It

Prioritizing prayer will bring you closer together and pave the way for God to work in your life and relationship. Use the following prayer as a jumping-off point.

Lord Jesus, you are the perfect example of serving. Thank you for giving your life for us. You laid down your life for us, and so we choose to lay down our lives for each other. Teach us to do nothing out of selfish ambition or vain conceit. We choose to humbly value and serve others with you as our example. In Jesus' name. Amen.

THE POOR, SICK, AND STRANGER

Truly I tell you, whatever you did for one of the least of these brothers and sisters of mine, you did for me.

Matthew 25:40

My children share my faith and hold to Scripture as their primary source of truth. They watch me like a hawk to make sure that my beliefs and behavior match the teachings of Jesus.

My daughter calls me Daddy, except when I break the law. In that case, she calls me Pastor Ted. If I roll through a stop sign, she says, "Nice rolling stop, Pastor Ted." From the passenger seat, she glances at the speedometer and asks, "How fast are ya going there, Pastor Ted?"

Our children are always watching, and they know better than anyone whether our actions, attitudes, and speech match what Jesus teaches.

In one of Jesus' parables (Matt. 25:31–46), he separates sheep from goats at the final judgment. It was typical in that day to herd sheep and goats together but separate them for shearing. The sheep are a metaphor for true believers, and the goats are a metaphor for those who reject Christ. When Jesus taught about the difference between those who would be saved and those who would not be, he said that true believers serve others, while unbelievers do not. Feeding the hungry, caring for the sick, and welcoming the stranger do not save you. But saved people feed the hungry, care for the sick, and welcome the stranger.

This parable does not answer the question "What must I do to be saved?" But it does answer the question "What must I do now that I am saved?"

I have pastored for more than twenty-five years, and in that time I have met a lot of joyless Christians. They have not come to understand that Christianity and discipleship cannot be boiled down to attending church, reading their Bibles, tithing, and avoiding big sins. Following Jesus is so much more than that.

Saved people enter into the suffering of others. Saved people sacrifice in an effort to ease the suffering of others.

Jesus says to the saved group, "I was hungry and you gave me something to eat, I was thirsty and you gave me something to drink, I was a stranger and you invited me in, I needed clothes and you clothed me, I was sick and you looked after me, I was in prison and you came to visit me" (vv. 35–36).

Then that group asks, "Lord, when did we see you hungry and feed you, or thirsty and give you something to drink? When did we see you a stranger and invite you in, or needing clothes and clothe you? When did we see you sick or in prison and go to visit you?" (vv. 37–39).

Jesus answers, "Truly I tell you, whatever you did for one of the least of these brothers and sisters of mine, you did for me" (v. 40).

Jesus cares for the marginalized, impoverished, and imprisoned, and he calls us to do the same. Some scholars believe that the "brothers and sisters" in this text refers to Jesus' disciples, who suffered for the message of the gospel. This is a call to ease their suffering.

Many couples think compatible personality traits and a "good match" will result in high levels of marital satisfaction. But do you want to know what is more powerful than the favorable blending of personalities? Simply stated, it is being on mission together. A couple with a common mission uses their personality differences to move toward their common goal together.

What would happen in your marriage if you both focused on others and their needs? When have you last sacrificed to meet someone else's need?

There is great joy in serving the needs of others. When a couple serves together to ease the suffering of others, they please God and grow closer not only to him but also to each other.

Let's TALK about It

Discuss the following questions together, today or throughout the week.

- When you pull up to a stoplight and see a panhandler requesting help, what is the first thought that runs through your head? What keeps you from helping them?
- Has anyone ever taken advantage of your help? Did it keep you from helping in the future?
- Are we moved by the stories we hear at church of needs being met? When we hear them, do we want to do more, or do we think that is enough?

Let's DO Something about It

In Galatians 6:10 we read, "Therefore, as we have opportunity, let us do good to all people, especially to those who belong to the family of believers."

This week, find someone in need in your church or community. Once you identify the need, decide together how you will meet that need. Do not overcomplicate it. Do not post it online. Proceed with humility, generosity, and discretion.

Let's PRAY about It

Prioritizing prayer will bring you closer together and pave the way for God to work in your life and relationship. Use the following prayer as a jumping-off point.

Father, your heart is for the hurting. You have compassion for those who are hungry, sick, and imprisoned. Give us hearts like yours. Call out the excuses that keep us from helping. Send us on mission to help someone this week. Show us the opportunity and give us the means to help. It is in Jesus' name that we ask these things. Amen.

Week 44

A REFRESHING HOME

My beloved is to me a cluster of henna blossoms
from the vineyards of En Gedi.

Song of Songs 1:14

In the Song of Songs, the Shulammite woman refers to En Gedi to describe the environment created around her king: "My beloved is to me a cluster of henna blossoms from the vineyards of En Gedi" (1:14). En Gedi is a lush desert oasis providing rest, rejuvenation, and relaxation to weary travelers. This biblical poetry paints a picture of a home that refreshes those who gather there.

Here are some practical ways in which couples create a refreshing home.

A refreshing home creates a judgment-free zone. While the home is a place where we sharpen one another, it should not be a place of criticism and critical spirits. If your role at work includes leadership or management, turn that off when you walk through the front door. Refreshing your marriage and family starts with being present, both physically and mentally. Though I am a pastor and teacher, my family does not need me to turn every moment into a sermon or staff meeting.

A refreshing home gives each other space. If you find yourself out of words and needing to unplug, find a quiet space and relax. One way to honor your marriage and family is to know when each person needs a few minutes to themselves. A great gift to bestow on someone is to say, "Why don't you take the next hour to yourself and enjoy some alone time?"

A refreshing home is one in which the members share one another's load. If you are the first one home at night, think of ways to help those who will arrive later. Pick up clothes lying around. Start a load of dishes or laundry. When our kids were young, we had a fun way of getting the chores done. Like a military drill, we declared five minutes of get-it-done tenacity. We ran around the house like mad picking stuff up, organizing, vacuuming, folding, wiping down, and sweeping. From the outside looking in, it would've looked hectic and out of control. To us, it was a fun, fast way to work together to complete the housework.

A refreshing home makes time for hobbies. All homes need trash picked up, laundry sorted, meals prepared, lawns mowed, and homework completed. The sooner you get your work done, the sooner you can relax. Extracurricular activities allow you to mentally break away from your job and school assignments. Every family needs a hobby that everyone enjoys. Hobbies create lifelong memories worth repeating.

The Herschend family of Branson, Missouri, founded Silver Dollar City more than fifty years ago. The mission statement for their theme park reads, "Creating memories worth repeating." Their desire is that parents will bring their children, and the whole family will leave wanting to come back next year. They hope the family's memories are so fond that the children will return with their own kids one day. Shared activities create close-knit families. Hobbies disconnect us from the daily grind, relieve the pressure of routine, and give us extra time to focus on one another.

Our family spends time each summer on the lake. My wife often comments, "I like it when we're out here because our minds are turned off. It's very healthy for our minds to be focused on other stuff." She is right.

Let's TALK about It

Discuss the following questions together, today or throughout the week.

At dinner tonight, ask your family the following questions and give everyone an opportunity to create a refreshing home:

- Have you ever hesitated about or dreaded coming home?
- When you walk through the door at night, what is the first thing you want to see or hear?
- If you could change one thing about our home to make it more refreshing, what would it be?

Let's DO Something about It

Plan an activity you can do as a couple or family in the next seven days. It needs to be refreshing. Use the list below to begin planning. If you or a member of your family is exhausted just thinking about it, cross it off the list. Come to a consensus on a refreshing activity and mark it on the calendar.

A refreshing activity around your home for everyone is (feel free to check more than one):

____ Movie night

____ Backyard camping

____ Board game

____ Walk around the neighborhood

____ Catch in the backyard

____ Declutter a closet

____ Pickleball in the driveway

____ Other _____

____ Other _____

____ Other _____

Let's PRAY about It

Prioritizing prayer will bring you closer together and pave the way for God to work in your life and relationship. Use the following prayer as a jumping-off point.

Lord, we can't run on fumes and expect to have a thriving relationship with you and each other. Fill us today. We choose to slow down, be quiet, and bask in your presence. We want more of you. Refresh us. We repent of the distractions that keep us from enjoying time with you. Help us to remove them and prioritize you, our marriage, and our family. In Jesus' name we pray. Amen.

STAYING CONNECTED WHEN FEELING ISOLATED, ANXIOUS, OR UNCERTAIN

*Relieve the troubles of my heart
and free me from my anguish.*

Psalm 25:17

When gripped by feelings of isolation, fear, anxiety, and uncertainty, turn to the Psalms. They remind us that we are not alone and that the Lord is ever present in the midst of dark seasons. We pour out our hearts to him. No need to mask our feelings with God. He knows what each one of us thinks and feels.

In Psalm 25:16–17, David cried out to God:

> Turn to me and be gracious to me,
>   for I am lonely and afflicted.
> Relieve the troubles of my heart
>   and free me from my anguish.

How often do you cry out to God like that? Having feelings of hurt, fear, or frustration does not make you a bad Christian. Express your pain to him. He listens and cares.

On March 15, 2020, the "first day of COVID-19," most businesses in our town shut down and physical gatherings were canceled. It was surreal walking into our empty church building and preaching to an empty room. What we thought would last a few weeks turned into a few months. I had no idea the toll this would take on me emotionally, physically, and relationally. As the weeks went on, I wore down.

As people lost their jobs, panic set in. Our children came home from school for spring break and never went back. City officials told us to avoid family and friends in hospitals and nursing homes. State and local restrictions kept us in our houses, leaving only to purchase essential items.

At the end of March, I walked into our church staff meeting and wrote the stages of the grief cycle on the whiteboard. We used these stages to work through the shutdown as the family of Woodland Hills Family Church:

> Stage 1—Shock and Denial (confusion and fear)
> Stage 2—Anger (frustration and irritation)
> Stage 3—Depression (feeling helpless and overwhelmed, and having low energy)
> Stage 4—Dialogue or Bargaining (reaching out, wanting to share feelings and story)
> Stage 5—Acceptance (developing a new plan)

The loss we experienced was grief. I shared with our staff Romans 12:15, "Rejoice with those who rejoice; mourn with those who mourn." Ministry in this season meant we mourned our collective losses. Our sermons, messaging, and tone during the shutdown needed to move with the stages of grief. Tone deafness is when a leader jumps to stage five and wants the church to already be in the place of acceptance, though everyone else is still in the other four stages.

With our grief came prolonged disconnection. We had technology to help, but talking to someone on a screen pales in comparison to gathering around a table and sharing a meal. As I told our congregation repeatedly, "I am grateful for technology and live streaming, but I long to gather face to face." I shared John's heart in 3 John 13–14: "I had much to write to you, but I would rather not write with pen and ink. I hope to see you soon, and we will talk face to face" (ESV).

In the midst of this crisis, isolation, and grief, we grew in our dependence on God and one another. We will always look back on 2020 as a great interruption, but also as a time of renewed connection and community.

Psalm 30:11 reminds us that some seasons in life bring great pain and loss, but the Lord can turn it to joy: "You turned my wailing into dancing; you removed my sackcloth and clothed me with joy."

Let's TALK about It

Discuss the following questions together, today or throughout the week.

- If you could describe the pandemic in one word, what would it be?
- How did the pandemic interrupt our rhythm as a couple?
- What was your greatest lesson coming out of that season?
- Since we all grieve at different paces, do you feel we give each other plenty of time to work through the stages of grief?

Let's DO Something about It

Every couple experiences loss at some point in their marriage. Think back to when you lost a loved one, job, or even a friendship. To better understand your spouse's grief cycle, reflect back on that loss and discuss with each other the time spent in each of the stages.

Stage 1—Shock and Denial (confusion and fear)

Stage 2—Anger (frustration and irritation)

Stage 3—Depression (feeling helpless and overwhelmed and having low energy)

Stage 4—Dialogue or Bargaining (reaching out, wanting to share feelings and story)

Stage 5—Acceptance (developing a new plan)

Let's PRAY about It

Prioritizing prayer will bring you closer together and pave the way for God to work in your life and relationship. Use the following prayer as a jumping-off point.

Father, you grieve with us. You walk with us through pain and loss. You never rush us, but you walk side by side with us through it all. Thank you for comforting us and bringing us greater joy. In Jesus' name. Amen.

Week 46

HOPE DEFERRED

Hope deferred makes the heart sick,
but a longing fulfilled is a tree of life.
Proverbs 13:12

Country music shaped my childhood. I know the lyrics of almost every classic country song of the 1980s and '90s.

My classmates and friends relentlessly ridiculed me for my taste in music. When they went to see Def Leppard at the Rosemont Horizon, I went to see Lee Greenwood at the DuPage County Fair.

Garth Brooks changed everything for me in high school. For some reason, he appealed to even my heavy metal friends. When his songs played at school dances, everyone sang along. Garth rescued my fragile sense of coolness at those dances.

The first time I saw Garth live was at the Grand Ole Opry in Nashville, Tennessee. That night, I knew I wanted to be a country music artist.

In a recent sermon on Proverbs 13:12, I shared with our church family the reality of dying to a dream. God takes the death of a dream and births something brand new in us. We look back years later and see his hand all over it.

My illustration in that sermon was my dream to perform on the stage of the Grand Ole Opry. Center stage at the Opry is a circle of wood taken from the stage at the Ryman Auditorium, where the Opry started in 1925. My dream through high school and college was to perform on that circle.

I told our church, "God had another plan for my life, and it did not include the Grand Ole Opry. I died to that dream, but God gave me plenty of other dreams that came true. What dream are you holding on to but you need to let go of? What is holding you back from a joy-filled life?"

The day after I gave that sermon, I heard from country music legend Larry Gatlin. Someone had tipped him off to my message, and he'd gone online to watch it. "Preacher," he said, "the next time me and the brothers play at the Opry, I want you to come up and join us on the last verse of 'All the Gold in California.'"

When I told our worship team about my big break the next Sunday, they shot down my soaring imagination. "You know they are not going to give you a microphone." God always puts someone in your life to keep you humble.

Nonetheless, I'm still waiting on my big day. It's the circle or bust!

God is always at work in your life. He is not done writing your story. You may be heartsick waiting for your dream house, dream job, or dream vacation. Your plans for all that may fall through—and that is okay. Dying to a dream makes the heart ache, yes, but do not forget the second half of the verse: "A longing fulfilled is a tree of life."

Not every dream comes true, but some do. God never wastes our hurts and heartache. He uses them in this season and the next to minister to others.

God did not waste my dream of playing at the Grand Ole Opry. He took my love of country music and called me to pastor in Branson, Missouri. Branson is where country music legends build theaters and play out their final years.

All those songs I listened to while riding in my dad's Plymouth Volare are now played live in my little town. Branson is my longing fulfilled.

By the way, Larry has not given me a date yet. Larry, if you are reading this, give me a call.

Let's TALK about It

Discuss the following questions together, today or throughout the week.

- What dream did you die to that you now see had to go away for you to be where you are today?
- What relationship did you walk away from, only to see how it made your marriage stronger?
- What dream job did you quit or not get, and you now see how it brought you to this very spot?
- What longing fulfilled brought your marriage great joy?

Let's DO Something about It

This week is not just about dying to a dream, but it is also about letting God birth new dreams in you. Make date night this week a dream date that gets your dreaming muscle working again. Allow it to portray a special future for your marriage.

Big dreams for down the road are vital, but so are smaller dreams you can pursue in the here and now. These more immediate dreams provide stepping stones to get you from one stressful day to the next. They keep you hopeful, while everything else is keeping you hoping.

Take these questions with you on the date to give your dream muscle a workout:

1. At this point in your life, which would you choose to make your life better: better physical health, better relationships, more money, or a different job?
2. If you could rewind to any point in your life, what would you want to relive? Would you leave it the same or change it?
3. If you could try out any occupation for a year, what would it be?
4. What would you do with $10 million dollars?
5. If you could take lessons to become an expert at anything, what would it be?
6. Hollywood called. They want to make a movie about you. What would it be about and who would play you?
7. If you could be a professional athlete, regardless of age or physical ability, what sport do you think you would enjoy the most?
8. Describe your dream house.

Let's PRAY about It

Prioritizing prayer will bring you closer together and pave the way for God to work in your life and relationship. Use the following prayer as a jumping-off point.

Father, we delight in knowing that you give us the desires of our hearts. We want our hearts aligned with yours. We want our desires to be your desires for us. Yes, we mourn the death of a dream, but we are filled with anticipation for what you will do next in our marriage. We praise you for giving us big dreams and aspirations. It is in Jesus' name that we pray. Amen.

Week 47

CHANGE OF PLANS

Many are the plans in a person's heart,
but it is the LORD's purpose that prevails.

Proverbs 19:21

The Bible is not opposed to planning. We are to plan but remain open to major course corrections. Not everything happens on our timetable or in the way we plan it. The Lord works out his purposes for our lives all along the way. There is great joy and rest found in surrendering to God's plan and purpose for our lives.

After I walked away from my dream of becoming a country music legend, I jumped headlong into government and politics. My dream shifted from the circle at the Grand Ole Opry to the Oval Office at the White House.

I planned everything about my college life so I would end up in our nation's capital. I majored in political science, served on every congressional campaign in our area, and applied for the most prestigious internships available.

My new dream began to come true at the beginning of my senior year. I received an offer to intern at the US Senate Republican Policy Committee, led by Senator Don Nickles from Oklahoma. It was a paid internship that almost guaranteed me a job in DC after college.

Amy was the reason for my only hesitation. We were not officially dating, but my chances looked good.

Sometime later, when Amy and I had begun dating in earnest, I was in the computer lab when the call came in. It was the director of the internship program. "Ted," he said, "I've got great news. You are one of two people I'm inviting to come work for us in DC for a year."

"Thank you for the opportunity," I said, "but I'm going to pass and stay on campus for my senior year."

The director of the program was shocked and annoyed. "No one declines this offer. Are you sure you want to do this?"

"Yes," I said and hung up. I had complete peace about the decision because I knew God had plans for Amy and me. Staying on campus was the best choice for dating and getting to know Amy better.

At the end of that year, I asked her to be my wife, and she said, "Yes!"

A month before she said yes, God took the desire for politics completely away from me. Dr. James Merritt preached a sermon at convocation, and God used it to call me into pastoral ministry.

I am grateful for God's plan and purpose working out in my life and marriage. Amy and I both look back over twenty-five years of marriage and rejoice in what God has done. But had I gone to DC for that year … who knows what my life would've been like?

We sing a worship song in church that makes me emotional every time. Two lines in the lyrics say, "All the glory and the honor to the Son…. I praise God for what He's done."[*]

---

* "What He's Done," by Kristian Stanfill, Jacob Sooter, Tasha Cobbs Leonard, Anna Golden, released January 3, 2022, on *Burn Bright* (Studio EP), Passion Music, Capitol CMG, Essential Music Publishing.

Never stop planning, but hold your plans with open hands. When plans change, our minds and hearts can fill with confusion, panic, frustration, and chaos. Choose to see God and his purposes at work in the change. Look back over big, unexpected course corrections in your life with praise, worship, gratefulness, and joy. May God be glorified in our lives and his plans for us.

Let's TALK about It

Discuss the following conversation starters and questions together, today or throughout the week.

- Share some of the emotions that hit you when plans change.
- Do we honor each other's plans by sticking to them the best we can?
- Is there something in your current plans that is not coming to fruition and frustrates you?
- What are some of the roadblocks in our current plans?
- What are some practical steps we can take to move from confusion, panic, frustration, and chaos to praise, worship, gratefulness, and joy?

Let's DO Something about It

Have you ever had anyone ask you for your five-year plan? Sometimes that question comes out of nowhere and catches us off guard. I have never answered that question well, but it does force me to ask great questions about the future.

In the space below, write one goal next to each category. Be specific and place a deadline on it. Keep in mind that the plan is loose and open to change.

Personal Goal:

Financial Goal:

Family Goal:

Vocational Goal:

Church Goal:

Let's PRAY about It

Prioritizing prayer will bring you closer together and pave the way for God to work in your life and relationship. Use the following prayer as a jumping-off point.

Father, you know what is best for us. Your purposes for our marriage include worshipping you, living like Jesus, serving others, fellowshipping with other believers, and sharing the good news with the lost. We plan according to your purposes. Guide our steps. Redirect our path when we stray from your purposes. Thank you for giving us guidance as we pursue your plan for our lives. We love you and ask these things in Jesus' name. Amen.

GOOD NEWS OF GREAT JOY

But the angel said to them, "Do not be afraid. I bring you
good news that will cause great joy for all the people."
Luke 2:10

We read it at Christmas but need it every day. The gospel is not only good news for the lost, but it is also the daily reminder for the Christian that the battle is won and victory is ours through Christ Jesus.

I grew up in a legalistic church. I spent most of my childhood feeling as though I never measured up to what God expected or wanted from me. When I was twenty, a college professor shared with me something that changed my life forever. "There is nothing you can do to make God love you more," he said, "and there is nothing you can do to make God love you less." A switch flipped that day, and I never again attempted to earn his love. He loves me unconditionally.

The fact is, "All have sinned and fall short of the glory of God" (Rom. 3:23). My sin separated me from God and brought on me the penalty of death. Romans 6:23 clearly states, "For the wages of sin is death, but the gift of God is eternal life in Christ Jesus our Lord." Jesus died for my sins and forever removed from me the penalty of death.

There's nothing I can do to earn salvation. Salvation-by-addition is the false teaching that says church attendance, tithing, serving at a mission, feeding the hungry, caring for the sick, and welcoming the stranger saves you. But those things do not save you. Nor does your family of origin, church, or denomination. Jesus alone saves. The gospel that saves us is the same gospel that reminds us that we do not earn eternal joy by our works.

Paul reminded the Ephesians:

> For it is by grace you have been saved, through faith—and this is not from yourselves, it is the gift of God—not by works, so that no one can boast. For we are God's handiwork, created in Christ Jesus to do good works, which God prepared in advance for us to do. (Eph. 2:8–10)

We are not saved *by* works but to *do* good works. Every morning when my feet hit the floor, I remind myself of the salvation I have in Christ. My day is not spent earning (or repaying the Lord for) his love, acceptance, and salvation. My day is about living in such a way that expresses thanks to him for all he has done for me.

God is patient. He is not mad at you. The psalmist rested in this truth: "But you, O Lord, are a God merciful and gracious, slow to anger and abounding in steadfast love and faithfulness" (Ps. 86:15 ESV). He is not out to get you. He sent his Son, Jesus, to die for you.

Salvation is found in no other name. Jesus is "the way and the truth and the life. No one comes to the Father except through" him (John 14:6).

Paul gave us the path to salvation in Jesus:

> If you declare with your mouth, "Jesus is Lord," and
> believe in your heart that God raised him from the
> dead, you will be saved. For it is with your heart
> that you believe and are justified, and it is with your
> mouth that you profess your faith and are saved....
> For, "Everyone who calls on the name of the Lord
> will be saved." (Rom. 10:9–10, 13)

Rest in the assurance of your salvation. Jesus saves you, loves you, and walks with you. This is good news of great joy.

Let's TALK about It

Discuss the following questions together, today or throughout the week.

- How old were you when you heard the gospel for the first time?
- Who shared it with you?
- When was the last time you shared your salvation testimony with someone?
- What passages do you turn to for reassurance of salvation?

Let's DO Something about It

Research tells us that most believers never share their faith or story of salvation. We fear rejection and not knowing what to say. Take some time this week to write down some details of your salvation story and corresponding verses. Pray for courage and share your story with at least one person in your circle of influence. After you share, invite them to receive Christ as Savior.

Let's PRAY about It

Prioritizing prayer will bring you closer together and will pave the way for God to work in your life and relationship. Use the following prayer as a jumping-off point.

Father, thank you for sending your Son to die for me. I receive him as my Savior and want to serve him all the days of my life. I want others to know of this free gift. Give me boldness and courage as I share this good news of great joy. It is in Jesus' name that we commit to you. Amen.

JOY-FILLED PARENTING

The father of a righteous child has great joy;
a man who fathers a wise son rejoices in him.
May your father and mother rejoice;
may she who gave you birth be joyful!

Proverbs 23:24–25

Parents rejoice when their children follow Jesus. The most important influence you have on your child is your love for the Lord. As you walk with Jesus, bring your children along with you. The Message Bible paraphrase says, "Fathers, don't frustrate your children with no-win scenarios. Take them by the hand and lead them in the way of the Master" (Eph. 6:4).

I remember taking my family to Times Square when our kids were young. The crowds overwhelmed my son. He reached for my hand and held it in a death grip. I provided safety as I led him through the sea of people. That is a simple word picture of how to parent the hearts of our children. We take their hand and walk alongside them through their childhood.

Every Christian parent I know wants well-behaved, successful, and responsible kids who love Jesus. We encourage, nurture, guide, and direct them to that end. However, if we are not careful, our motives get out of whack and our kids spend their childhood fulfilling Mom's and Dad's desires and dreams. In doing so, they are delayed in discovering who God created them to be and what he has prepared for them to do. When parents push their personal agendas, rooted in performance, the kids have a hard time identifying their God-given personality, passions, and pursuits.

My grandparents' generation's primary concern was providing food, shelter, clothes, and education for their children. These basic needs drove them to their knees in prayer. Kids were not the center of the home but rather welcome additions who were expected to work hard to do their part. Instilling responsibility and duty was a primary goal of this generation's parenting style.

Around the 1980s, parents became more encouraging, nurturing, and hovering. Instead of "Three strikes and you're out," we allowed kids to stay in the batter's box for as long as it took for them to connect with the ball. We did not want them to feel like losers. Gold stars on every school paper boosted their self-esteem. Excessive praise for every attempt and ribbons for each competition, regardless of winning or even completing, helped them feel like winners.

This led parents to obsess over achievement and success, looking for big moments on the stage and field. We tended to use our children's accomplishments and attributes to impress others. We created environments for our kids to succeed, rather than teaching them to succeed in environments or situations they cannot control.

We accelerated the childhood milestones with toddler reading programs and organized preschool sports leagues. Then later, we delayed the adulthood milestones of leaving home, finishing education, getting employment, finding a spouse, and starting a family. We centered the home around the children, prolonging their adolescence with too much privilege and not enough responsibility.

All of this led parents to take too much credit and too much blame for the way their children turned out. Parenting comes with pressure, responsibility, heartache, joy, and frustration. We have to learn to delete the narrative that kept repeating, "It's too late" and "It's my fault."

If you want to experience greater joy as a parent, stop feeding your regrets and ask Jesus to redeem your remaining days. Parent with the end in mind. If the goal of parenting is to raise children who love and follow Jesus, then direct your efforts to that end. When they've grown, we want to be able to say, "I have no greater joy than to hear that my children are walking in the truth" (3 John 4 ESV).

Remember, there is no such thing as a perfect parent. That means we cannot expect perfect children. Give yourself permission to learn and grow same way you want your child to learn and grow.

Let's TALK about It

Discuss the following questions together, today or throughout the week.

- What is the most challenging part of parenting?
- Do you have any regrets as a parent?
- Do (or did) we use the attributes and accomplishments of our children to impress others?
- Do (or did) we set our expectations too high for our children?
- Are (or were) we intentional with expressing our love for the Lord and guiding our children in it?

Let's DO Something about It

Gather your children or grandchildren around the table this week. Zoom or FaceTime if they live far away. Maybe invite them to join you for a brief time of Bible reading and prayer. Perhaps you might share a devotional that you have read in this book. Tell them your faith story and something that the Lord has taught you recently. Never underestimate your influence in the lives of your children and grandchildren.

Let's PRAY about It

Prioritizing prayer will bring you closer together and pave the way for God to work in your life and relationship. Use the following prayer as a jumping-off point.

Father, I am not the perfect parent, but you are the perfect Father. I look to you for strength and guidance in raising our children. We will not feed regrets but will ask that you redeem our remaining days. Our children are still watching and listening, and we want to lead them well. We pray these things in Jesus' matchless name. Amen.

WELCOME TO THE EMPTY NEST

*I am reminded of your sincere faith, which first lived
in your grandmother Lois and in your mother Eunice
and, I am persuaded, now lives in you also.*

2 Timothy 1:5

My dear friend Dr. Jim Burns says, "When your child leaves home and their life fills up with fresh experiences, follow their lead."

When our first child left home, I was numb for a month. Amy caught me wandering aimlessly around our home and was gracious in her question, "Are you okay?" She did not expect an answer but wanted me to know she noticed and cared.

We grieved at different paces in the first month or two of the empty nest. And yes, it was grief. We were grappling with the fact that we'd lost one season of life and were having to learn to accept a new season. It was not a bad loss, but it was loss.

Sonya Hayter was one of my favorite church members because she had a great sense of humor. She dished it out as well as she received it. We joked with each other a lot before and after services, and I counted on her for a debrief of my sermon.

Sonya was familiar with my teaching and my jokes about children leaving home. She laughed along at those jokes … until her last child left home. Then she approached me the Sunday after they'd dropped her daughter off at college. "In today's sermon," she said, "I don't want to hear any snarky comments about the empty nest." She was serious and emotional. I heeded her request and steered clear of the topic.

A few months later, around Thanksgiving, she came up to me with a big smile on her face and said, "Hey, Ted, I just want you to know that I am completely healed and enjoying the empty nest. Doug and I are great!"

Sonya needed time. That's the first lesson for all of us in the empty nest or entering it soon. Give yourself and your spouse grace as you enter this new season. Be patient.

The empty nest is a new season to rethink about each other. Youth sports no longer rule your life. School schedules are irrelevant. And you have more time to think about each other. Give each other thought time. Ask each other great questions. Find out what the other one is thinking. This is a great season to rediscover each other's passions and dreams for the future.

Approach this new season with a new fervor for the Lord and each other. Use this time to get serious about your spiritual influence with your adult children, and begin looking forward to one day influencing your grandchildren. I often remind the grandparents at our church, "You are living in your most influential season of life. Do not waste it. Do not squander it."

Your kids are still watching and learning. When they stop by for a visit, talk about the Lord "when you sit at home and when you walk along the road, when you lie down and when you get up"

(Deut. 6:7). You poured so much into your kids while they lived with you, and everything you say and do after they leave home reinforces that message.

The apostle Paul reminded young Timothy of the profound influence of our parents and grandparents: "I am reminded of your sincere faith, which first lived in your grandmother Lois and in your mother Eunice and, I am persuaded, now lives in you also" (2 Tim. 1:5).

Amy and I love and miss our kids. We are so glad we prioritized marriage in the home while we raised our kids and did not wait to enjoy life together after they left. Corynn and Carson see us living with the same intention and passion for each other now as we had when they were with us.

We may slow down with age, but we will not surrender influence. The empty nest is a new season with plenty of joy, both now and in the future.

Let's TALK about It

Discuss the following questions together, today or throughout the week.

- What do you fear most about the empty nest?
- What do you look forward to most about the empty nest?
- Can you think of a couple who thrived in the empty nest?
- What changed about their marriage after the kids left home?
- How would you describe their relationship with their adult children and/or grandchildren?

Let's DO Something about It

Let's plan a double date with an empty-nest couple who inspires us. Use the following conversation to lead the date and learning:

- How did you meet?
- How old were you when you married?
- Can you describe your feelings in the first month after your last child left home?
- How often do you talk to your kids?
- Do they ever ask for your advice?
- Have you ever been in trouble for offering unsolicited advice? If so, what steps did you take to repair the relationship?
- What's the hardest part of the empty nest? Best part?

Let's PRAY about It

Prioritizing prayer will bring you closer together and pave the way for God to work in your life and relationship. Use the following prayer as a jumping-off point.

Father, we ask that you give us the strength in our second half of life and marriage to influence our family well. As our strength fades, we rely even more on the strength that you and your Word give us. Bless our children and grandchildren. May they follow you all the days of their life. We ask these things in the name of your Son, Jesus. Amen.

LOVE FOR A LIFETIME

Let no debt remain outstanding, except the continuing debt to love one another, for whoever loves others has fulfilled the law.

Romans 13:8

How do we measure our love for one another? One book we read countless times to our kids when they were young was *I Love You to the Moon and Back*. That title became an expression in our home. We took it so far that we painted a mural of it on our daughter's bedroom wall.

After bedtime reading, we asked our kids, "How much do Mom and Dad love you?"

"To the moon and back!" they answered.

With outstretched arms, I asked, "Do I love you this much?"

The answer is always yes, but that does not come close to describing the love I have for them. My arms can't stretch that far.

Romans 13:8 proclaims that love is a debt we never pay off. Though we do not earn salvation and we never have to pay God back for his gift of eternal life, we still owe a sort of debt to endlessly pass God's love along to others. You can pay off your car or your house, but you never pay off love. We will never get to a point in our marriage where we can say, "I've loved enough. I'm done now." If you think you have exhausted love, keep loving. You have a ways to go.

When I hear a spouse say, "We fell out of love," what I hear is, "For whatever reason, we stopped deciding to love each other." Marital drift leads to a lack of love.

Romans 13:9 says, "The commandments, 'You shall not commit adultery,' 'You shall not murder,' 'You shall not steal,' 'You shall not covet,' and whatever other command there may be, are summed up in this one command: 'Love your neighbor as yourself.'" We are not commanded to love ourselves, because we already know how to do that. In other words, I know how to care for myself and meet my needs. Love is caring for my spouse with the same intention and enthusiasm with which I care for myself.

Amy calls me out when I compare my physical health to that of others. I often point out people I see who are in worse shape than I am in order to feel better about my eating or (lack of) physical exercise. Amy is right that this is a terrible strategy for achieving confidence.

We do this with our sin too. We say to ourselves, "I am not as bad as he is." "I don't talk about others behind their backs like she does." "He eats or drinks way more than I do." Comparing your sin to another's is a terrible strategy for growing in Jesus.

The same is true with love. Our source is Jesus, not ourselves or others. First John 4:15–16 says, "If anyone acknowledges that Jesus is the Son of God, God lives in them and they in God. And so we know and rely on the love God has for us. God is love. Whoever lives in love lives in God, and God in them."

Abiding in God's love requires that I know and rely on his love. My love fails, but his never does. My love wears out, but his continues forever. "Give thanks to the LORD, for he is good; his love endures forever" (Ps. 107:1).

May you take the love of Jesus and use it to love your spouse with great joy until the Lord returns or calls one of you home.

Let's TALK about It

Discuss the following questions together, today or throughout the week.

- Name a few reasons people stop loving one another.
- Can you think of a couple who is still crazy in love even after having been married more than fifty years? How do they inspire you?
- What are some ways that any couple's love is on display?
- How can we better display our love for each other? Is there a practical step we can take toward this in the coming days or weeks?

Let's DO Something about It

Read through these traditional wedding vows. While these might not have been your wedding vows, consider the commitment to love expressed in them. Take turns reciting them to each other.

> I, _____, take you, _____,
> to be my wife/husband,
> to love you from this day forward,
> for better, for worse,
> for richer, for poorer,
> in sickness and in health,
> until the Lord returns
> or calls one of us home.
> In the name of the Father, Son, and Holy Spirit.

Let's PRAY about It

Prioritizing prayer will bring you closer together and pave the way for God to work in your life and relationship. Use the following prayer as a jumping-off point.

Father, Jesus is the measure of our love. We rely on him alone as our source. Help us love one another as Christ loves us. Help us care for each other as Christ cares for us. May we value each other and show grace to one another as you have shown it to us. We thank you for the love of Christ, and it is in his name that we pray these things. Amen.

HELPING EACH OTHER CROSS THE FINISH LINE

For I am already being poured out like a drink offering, and the time for my departure is near. I have fought the good fight, I have finished the race, I have kept the faith. Now there is in store for me the crown of righteousness, which the Lord, the righteous Judge, will award to me on that day—and not only to me, but also to all who have longed for his appearing.

2 Timothy 4:6–8

In this passage, Paul is not talking about leaving a city. Rather, his race on earth (his life) is ending, and he longs to be face to face with Jesus. This departure stirred up tension for Paul. In Philippians 1:23–24, he said, "I am torn between the two: I desire to depart and be with Christ, which is better by far; but it is more necessary for you that I remain in the body." He longed for heaven but knew his race on earth was not yet complete. He had more to do.

Finishing strong and receiving the victor's crown was his goal. Paul wanted that for you and me too.

Do you not know that in a race all the runners run,
but only one gets the prize? Run in such a way as to

get the prize. Everyone who competes in the games goes into strict training. They do it to get a crown that will not last, but we do it to get a crown that will last forever. (1 Cor. 9:24–25)

We run this race until we draw our last breath. We run for the crown.

You are not done with your race when the kids leave home or you retire from your job. The finish line is at the end of this life's journey. Until that day comes, run. When the race is hard and you are out of breath, run. When you hit the wall, keep running until you cross the finish line.

One aspect of Paul's race that inspires me is that he did not run alone. He did not fight the good fight by himself. Paul surrounded himself with others who loved and cared for him as he poured into them.

In Colossians 4, we read a list of teammates who surrounded Paul: Tychicus, Onesimus, Aristarchus, Mark, Jesus who is called Justus, Epaphras, Luke, and Demas are all mentioned in verses 7–14. Paul uses words like *dear brother, faithful minister, fellow servant in the Lord,* and *coworkers for the kingdom of God* to describe these men. In verse 11, he says, "they have proved a comfort to me." This sentiment was a result of Paul's team supporting him while he was imprisoned in Rome.

Just like Paul, you do not need to run your race alone. No one expects you to fight the good fight by yourself. Now more than ever, you need a good support team. Who is on your team? Who is cheering you on today? I encourage you to take a moment and write down the names of the friends and family members who you know are with you until the end … or until they cross the finish line. Give them a call and check in on them. Be an encouragement.

Caring for one another and carrying each other's burdens is when the church is at its best.

If you have hit a wall, now is the time to reach out for help. In Galatians 6:2, Paul exhorts the church to "carry each other's burdens, and in this way you will fulfill the law of Christ." We all have individual loads we must carry, but sometimes the load becomes too heavy for one person. When this happens, we need someone else to walk alongside us and help. That does not mean we drop our share of the load. It just means we need a little assistance. Caring for one another and carrying each other's burdens is when the church is at its best.

Some of the most inspirational moments in sports history have come when runners helped each other cross the finish line. We see the best in athletes when they stop near the end of a race to help a weary or injured runner.

Possibly the most memorable assist came during the 1992 Summer Olympics in Barcelona, Spain. British sprinter Derek Redmond was favored to medal in the 400 meters, but right in the middle of his semifinal race, his hamstring tore. That did not stop him from finishing the race. His father ran down to help him cross the finish line. If you watch the video, you cannot help but choke up as Derek wraps his arm around his dad and places his head on his shoulder. This illustration is a beautiful picture of the church and our call to help each other finish the race.

I pray you "run with perseverance the race marked out for us" (Heb. 12:1). Run hard, and help others finish strong. Lean on others to help you cross your finish line. We may change our pace, but we will not quit the race.

Let's TALK about It

Discuss the following questions together, today or throughout the week.

- What makes you want to quit the race?
- Who or what helps you to keep running?
- How can I best cheer you on as you run your race?
- Who has helped us run our race? How has their encouragement and support positively impacted our marriage?

Let's DO Something about It

On your date night this week, include a brisk walk in your plans. Shoot for walking somewhere new. Ask the above questions as you walk. Keep it light and fun. Consider all the ways you will support each other in your sunset years. Picture a special future for your marriage.

Let's PRAY about It

Prioritizing prayer will bring you closer together and pave the way for God to work in your life and relationship. Use the following prayer as a jumping-off point.

Father, give us strength and perseverance to run the race until the very end. We may tire and need a break, but let it be just that: a break. We want to run until the very end. Our finish line is when we are in your presence. In Jesus' name. Amen.

Thank you for investing the last 52 weeks in Greater Joy TWOgether. *Amy and I plan on giving the rest of our lives to helping couples enjoy life together. We hope and pray this book outlives us. We also pray that the joy in your marriage will be so infectious that your children and grandchildren will experience the same joy in theirs. I am cheering you on!*